# SpringerBriefs in Computer Science

W0079081

More information about this series at http://www.springer.com/series/10028

Rae Earnshaw

# State of the Art in Digital Media and Applications

 Springer

Rae Earnshaw
Centre for Visual Computing, Faculty
    of Engineering and Informatics
University of Bradford
Bradford, UK

School of Creative Arts
Wrexham Glyndŵr University
Wrexham, UK

ISSN 2191-5768                    ISSN 2191-5776    (electronic)
SpringerBriefs in Computer Science
ISBN 978-3-319-61408-3            ISBN 978-3-319-61409-0    (eBook)
DOI 10.1007/978-3-319-61409-0

Library of Congress Control Number: 2017945920

Printed on acid-free paper

This Springer imprint is published by Springer Nature
The registered company is Springer International Publishing AG
The registered company address is: Gewerbestrasse 11, 6330 Cham, Switzerland

After looking in Chap. 3 at how digital media technology often arises as collaborations across many fields, both technical and artistic, and how those partnerships, especially with small and medium enterprises (SMEs), are important for that process, in Chap. 4, the evolution of digital imaging is detailed starting with traditional analog photography to today's streaming media techniques that inherently rely on digital technology for their robustness and ubiquitous presence.

Digital libraries are discussed in Chap. 5 and used as a springboard to introduce important social issues such as the need for reliable archives, the effect on organizations and institutions (libraries, museums, exhibitions, and conferences) that traditionally were the repositories and gatekeepers for information, the evolving nature of copyright, and the blurring of traditional distinctions between content creators, publishers, broadcasters, and consumers.

With these preliminaries dealt with, Chap. 6 looks at the many applications of digital media that combine specific types of media content with innovative interaction techniques and mechanisms for distributing and sharing digital media and a more in-depth discussion of the blurring of traditional roles within media. For many readers, this will be the main point of the book, but the earlier material provides the context within which to understand how these applications arose and why those that have been successful are a consequence of the historical processes that led us to where we are now.

Chapter 7 focuses on the phenomenon of social media, and enabling Web 2.0 / Enterprise 2.0, that has driven the most pervasive and profound political, cultural, and artistic consequences of the global digital revolution. Chapter 8 explores future implications but with a cautionary warning that just as many of the visionary ideas discussed in Chap. 2 took decades to realize – and some of the visions turned out to be wrong – all that we can really predict is that the legal, economic, and social frameworks that have been stressed by the emergence of digital media will continue to need adjustment as even newer technologies and the applications they enable become commonplace.

Continuing the practice of "drill down" he adopted in his first three books in the series, for each chapter, Rae provides additional references to further reading that go beyond the discussions in the main text. There is also a bibliography at the end of the book that lists even more related literature. This allows an interested reader to look more deeply at topics of particular interest.

Vancouver, Canada                                                          Kellogg S. Booth
April 2017

# Foreword

Anyone familiar with the changes that digital media has brought about in our everyday lives will want to learn more about what is driving the changes – the myriad of computer-based applications that are built on digital media technologies and are designed to meet a variety of social, cultural, economic, and artistic needs that are rapidly evolving. Rae Earnshaw's newest book, *State of the Art in Digital Media and Applications*, is a good place to start for a comprehensive look at how emerging digital media technologies are being used in a variety of application domains that are transforming how we create, consume, exchange, and manipulate media content.

This is Rae's fourth book in a series that focuses on digital media and creativity. The first book, *Research and Development in Art, Design and Creativity*, looked at the roles collaboration and communication play in research and development in creative fields such as art and design and especially the increasing importance of technological tools to support that activity. The second book, *Research and Development in the Academy, Creative Industries and Applications*, focused on university research and its relationship broadly with industry applications and specifically in the creative industries. The third book, *Art, Design and Technology: Collaboration and Implementation*, examined how art, design, and technology intertwine in the production of digital media applications. This fourth book steps back to look at the broader landscape of digital media applications by first summarizing the convergence of information technologies (computers and computer programming), telecommunications (including the Internet and the World Wide Web), and traditional media as it has evolved into new media or, as it is more often referred to, digital media.

Following the introductory Chap. 1, where the elements of digital media and related technology are summarized, Chap. 2 is a brief triptych of important visionary ideas that emerged from the early days of computing, electronic communication, and technological advances in media and provides insight into the possibilities that were imagined when digital media as we know it today was still many decades in the future.

# Preface

The first book[1] in this subject area covered the key aspects of collaboration and communication in research and development (R & D) and how technology may be used to support creativity in the R & D process. The second book[2] covered the collaboration between the academy and industry to support developments in the creative industries and more general industrial applications. The third book[3] covered collaboration and implementation between art and design and technology.

This book examines the more general area of digital media as a whole and the application areas in which digital media is currently involved. Thus it is more of an overview and state-of-the-art survey of the field and examines the history of computing and the historical key visions in computing that have led to this current point in time and the current technologies being utilized in digital media. Current research issues in digital media are not presented or discussed in any detail in this book. A further volume is currently proposed to address the research and development agenda within the field of digital media.

There is insufficient space in a brief book of this nature to provide full detail of any particular area, and, where relevant, the more detailed material in the further reading and references at the end of each chapter is for readers to gain more detail where they feel they need it. There is also a bibliography at the end of the book with further reading grouped into sections to enable readers to easily find the further material which would be useful to them. This bibliography does not duplicate the further reading sections at the end of each chapter, so readers are advised to look at these first for further reading in the topic areas of the chapters and to use the bibliography for more general, and also more detailed, reading across the field of digital media.

---

[1] Earnshaw, R.A.: Research and Development in Art, Design and Creativity. Springer (2016) http://dx.doi.org/10.1007/978-3-319-33005-1

[2] Earnshaw, R.A.: Research and Development in the Academy: Creative Industries and Applications. Springer (2017) DOI 10.1007/978-3-319-54081-8

[3] Earnshaw, R.A.: Art, Design and Technology: Collaboration and Implementation. Springer (2017)

In this state-of-the-art review, the theoretical, practical, and technical aspects of digital media are examined. The increasing power of hardware and software technologies enables multiple data types to be processed with increasing ease and facility. From the web and computer games to mobile technologies and social media, digital media continues to develop and advance.

The convergence of IT, telecommunications, and media is bringing about a revolution in the way information is collected, stored, and accessed. There are three principal reasons why this is happening – reducing cost, increasing quality, and increasing bandwidth.

A wide range of applications such as computer games, multimedia production, animation, graphics and video editing, and digital video film making are examined in general terms only. These topics fall more within the generally accepted definition of creative industries, and these are covered in more detail in the second book which examines this area.

Media content is now created in digital form and can be repurposed across different media types such as DVD, Internet, or traditional print. This offers scope for different forms of advertising and providing added value to consumers by providing dynamic links to other relevant information. This provides new value chains and ecosystems. This in turn affects social and cultural contexts and interacts with them. The user such as content creator, publisher, and broadcaster is challenging and changing the traditional roles of news media, publishers, and entertainment corporations. This in turn changes social and governmental structures and affects their power, influence, and cultural impact.

This revolution is having effects on the development, organization, and distribution of information and artifact repositories such as libraries, museums, exhibitions, and conferences and the way in which physical and digital aspects are mediated to users. There are also current issues in ensuring that digital archives remain accessible to users into the long-term future and are not rendered obsolete by future shifts in technology. The changes that digital media and digital convergence are bringing about are substantial and are also likely to be long-lasting.

The University of Bradford, UK, pioneered the area of digital media in the mid-1990s by tripartite collaborations between technology, art and design, and media and broadcasting. It was done by setting up a new academic department because it did not sit easily within existing academic disciplines and structures. It was very successful in attracting students and also meeting the needs and requirements of the industry. It also highlighted the benefits and advantages of interdisciplinary collaborations. Involvement in a number of large interdisciplinary European projects over the years at the Universities of Leeds and Bradford required research and development in a number of application areas, such as multimedia assets for design, collaborative visualization over networks, and virtual entertainment, and led to a number of important results. These are detailed in the first book referred to above.

Involvement as a professor in the School of Creative Arts at Wrexham Glyndwr University, Wales, over recent years has provided opportunity to think about these aspects and publish a number of papers in collaboration with the faculty.

The book is being published in the SpringerBriefs series which are summaries of the state of the art in a particular area. It is being published as a print book, a Kindle book, and an e-book. In the latter, each chapter will be downloadable separately. This is why the further reading and references appear at the end of each chapter. Thus a chapter contains the main points in the area and the reasons for their significance. It is not intended to examine each of these points in detail – there is insufficient space to do this. However, the interested reader can follow up in the further reading or references for further detail and information.

It is hoped that this book makes a useful contribution to an important area of discussion and debate.

## Acknowledgments

Thanks and appreciation are due to all those who read draft versions of the chapters and provided comments to improve the technical content and readability. However, responsibility for the final text rests with the author.

Thanks are expressed to colleagues and students at the School of Creative Arts at Wrexham Glyndwr University, Wales, for the many useful discussions.

Thanks are expressed to Professor Kellogg Booth from the University of British Columbia, Canada, for providing the foreword to the book.

Thanks and appreciation are also due to Springer for the assistance and support with the production of the book and e-book.

Bradford, UK                                                                              Rae Earnshaw
April 2017

# Contents

# Chapter 1
# Introduction and Background

**Abstract** The development of digital media is reviewed and definitions are provided. The advantages of digital media over traditional media are set out, and the current challenges are summarized.

The convergence of IT, telecommunications, and media is bringing about a revolution in the way information is collected, stored and accessed. There are three principal reasons why this is happening – reducing cost, increasing quality, and increasing bandwidth. Digital media preserves content accuracy (e.g. digital television) in a way other systems do not. High bandwidth transmission from one place to another on the planet is now possible. Information is ubiquitous and globally accessible, and can be held and accessed just as easily on a global network as on a local personal computer or in a local library. Thus anyone generating state of the art content can produce an impact on the global network. Devices are increasingly intelligent and are network-ready. User interfaces are becoming more adaptable and flexible, and can be tailored to particular application domains. Digital intelligence is becoming seamless and invisible, enabling more attention to be paid to the content and the user's interaction with it.

Digital media includes a wide range of applications such as computer games, multimedia production, animation, graphics and video editing, and digital video film making. Media content is now created in digital form and can be repurposed across different media types such as DVD, Internet, or traditional print. This offers scope for different forms of advertising, and providing added value to consumers by providing dynamic links to other relevant information. This provides new value chains and ecosystems. This is turn affects social and cultural contexts, and interacts with them. The user as content creator, publisher, and broadcaster is changing the traditional roles of news media, publishers, and entertainment corporations. This in turn changes social and governmental structures and affects their power, influence, and cultural impact.

**Keywords** Digital convergence • Digital content creation • User as content creator • Value chains • Social and cultural impact • Hyperlinks • Digital integration

© The Author(s) 2017

R. Earnshaw, *State of the Art in Digital Media and Applications*, SpringerBriefs in Computer Science, DOI 10.1007/978-3-319-61409-0_1

## 1.1   Introduction

> When things are digital, they're all 1's and zero's, and so they commingle in ways we didn't
> anticipate and you could do things that were not like publishing or television, or computers,
> but were some intersection of those and that got known to be convergence, so between the
> switching, or trading of places and the convergence, you have today's media.
>   When we ship our laptop, we ship 1.6 million books with it. You can access free, 1.6
> million books and embedded in the laptop are 100 books per laptop of the choosing of the
> country, but what's important about that is, when you ship 100 laptops into a village, there
> are 100 different books on each of the laptops, so the village now has 10,000 books in the
> village and 1.6 million accessible. That's—that is really, really different.
>   So, to compare books to computers, I mean, computers are the way to get books. That is
> the medium for distributing text because it doesn't require paper, it doesn't—you know, it's
> editable. Nothing goes out of date, nothing goes out of print, it can be refreshed and
> updated. Negroponte [1].

Moore's Law [2, 3] results in ever-decreasing costs of processing, storage, and transmission. Over a period of 1.5 years functionality doubles for the same cost. Thus means that processing power, storage and transmission speeds double. This also includes the power of sensors and the number of pixels in displays and digital cameras. This has enabled computers and networks to handle more complex data types such as audio, video and animation just as easily as numbers and text. Moore's law brings about both technological and social change, as the technology results in impacts on society and produces shifts in the way consumers perceive and utilize the technology in an increasing variety of application domains (e.g. e-books, digital cameras, Facebook, Twitter).

## 1.2   Definitions of Media and Digital Media

Traditional media in the pre-digital era included print (such as news, magazines, and books), recordings, advertising, photography, art and analogue broadcast. These include components such as text, images, video, animation, film, and audio tape.

Digital media includes all forms of media information and data which is created, distributed, and received in digital form, such as print (for example, news, magazines, and books), recordings, advertising, photography, art and analogue broadcast. These include components such as text, images, video, and animation. It could also apply to digital content produced by any form of digital computer (such as PC, laptop, tablet, or mobile phone), and also more general digital devices for particular application domains such as digital cameras, simulators, virtual environments. It could also include more specialized forms of turnkey systems for medical applications such as MRI, CT, and PET scanners. Multimedia is where a particular set of data and communications may include multiple forms of information content (e.g. text, images, and video).

Digital media preserves content accuracy (e.g. digital television) in a way other systems do not. High bandwidth transmission from one place to another on the planet is now possible. Information is ubiquitous and globally accessible, and can be held and accessed just as easily on a global network as on a local personal computer or in a local library. Thus anyone generating state of the art content can produce an impact on the global network.

## 1.3  Origins of Digital Media

Digital media can trace its conceptual origins to a publication by Vannevar Bush in 1945 [4]. He envisioned a system of devices that would help professionals to store, analyze and communicate information. He termed it the "memex" a combination of "memory" and "index", able to store and index all human records, books and communications. The memex would give an "enlarged intimate supplement to one's memory" –

> *The owner of the memex, let us say, is interested in the origin and properties of the bow and arrow. Specifically he is studying why the short Turkish bow was apparently superior to the English long bow in the skirmishes of the Crusades. He has dozens of possibly pertinent books and articles in his memex. First he runs through an encyclopedia, finds an interesting but sketchy article, leaves it projected. Next, in a history, he finds another pertinent item, and ties the two together. Thus he goes, building a trail of many items. Occasionally he inserts a comment of his own, either linking it into the main trail or joining it by a side trail to a particular item. When it becomes evident that the elastic properties of available materials had a great deal to do with the bow, he branches off on a side trail which takes him through textbooks on elasticity and tables of physical constants. He inserts a page of longhand analysis of his own. Thus he builds a trail of his interest through the maze of materials available to him* [4].

Although the memex was never created, it was nevertheless very far sighted. This conceptual system of devices contains early intimations of the links between relevant items of information (such as was eventually realized as hyperlinks in the World Wide Web); digital repositories and encyclopedias (such as was eventually implemented by Wikipedia); and new ways of working together resulting in human insight, discovery, and scholarship (such as was eventually implemented in email and social media). It is clear that all these elements have had a significant transformative effect on the digital environment and how it is created, accessed, and used. Various papers and conferences have analyzed the extent to which these early ideas have facilitated development and progress [5–9].

## 1.4  Implications of Digital Media

Digital media has the following advantages over traditional media [10] –

- Opportunity to repurpose content to suit different kinds of receiving devices (e.g. to optimize on screen size and aspect ratio, and other ergonomic factors of the devices)
- Opportunity to adapt content for different sets of readers and constituencies with different interests.

- Such tailoring of the content can lead to greater personalization, impact and engagement with the reader and user – so it is of particular interest to all those companies engaged in the sales and marketing of products and services, as it can support relationship building between supplier and user.
- Opportunity to generate a real-time stream of content.
- Opportunity to directly interact with the content.
- Opportunity to provide a digital link within the content to other related content (the so-called hyperlink).
- Easier to integrate with other digital documents.

Digital media has the following disadvantages over traditional media –

- Long term preservation and archiving of content so that is still readable by a future generation, in thousands of years' time (as has been the case with many early written manuscripts in history).

Consequently digital media has had a disruptive effect on traditional media and, more particularly, on the hierarchies in the industry that have been established over many years to support the creation and delivery of information. Such hierarchies may no longer be appropriate for optimum creation for content and delivering it in a more personal, targeted, and interactive way in the new information age. In addition, the user is no longer a passive recipient of passive and fixed information, but is able to contribute their own information. Traditional broadcasting supported an information distribution model of 'from one to many' and reflected the editor's view of the information being transmitted. The Internet supports an information distribution of 'many to one' and 'many to many'. Items of news can be released by users in near real-time on the Internet without any delay or pre-filtering by traditional news media. It is not surprising therefore that this caused an impact of seismic proportions to traditional media industries. Some have sought to evaluate how best to move to digital media, or alternatively, to seek to combine traditional media with new media in order to get the benefits of both worlds.

Digital media faces the following challenges –

- Difficulties with traditional copyright and intellectual property laws which have been established in the context of traditional print media. This has partly resulted in the open content movement where authors and contributors to content are provided with opportunities to share their work with whoever wishes to utilize it, so foregoing their legal rights.
- The impact on social traditions and norms that have become well-established by traditional media.
- Addressing the issue of the digital divide – where there is an economic and social inequality between those who can easily access new media and those who cannot [11] – often the elderly who have had no training in the skills required to use digital devices, or those in the third world who cannot afford them. However, various initiatives are seeking to address these issues (e.g. town councils running evening classes for the elderly on computing – for the former; and the one laptop per child initiative for the latter [12]).

## 1.5  Creating and Using Digital Media

Constructing a digital media document offers the opportunity to create a linear story with associated digital hyperlinks to more detailed papers, articles and books which provide more detail on the history or on particular details of the story. It thus offers the opportunity for the reader to drill down into particular items of interest by using the links. It is therefore also a hierarchy of information as well as a linear one. This book is an example of such a digital media product. It offers a linear story in the printed book, but it also offered as an e-book with all the chapters unbundled. They can therefore be downloaded separately by the reader and read on their preferred digital device connected to the Internet. The hyperlinks can also be accessed directly on the device. Readers can therefore go more directly to the specialist information they need, without the overhead of having to read through information that they may not need.

Digital media may also be used as tools to analyze and deliver information or data in the context of today's challenges which include areas such as cybersecurity, big data, computational analytics, visual analytics, and new interaction paradigms including mixed reality and adaptive learning.

Trump has used Twitter messages to circumvent political control of news information disseminated by traditional media. Previous presidents have also sought to use the latest technological tools in their eras to communicate with the general problem as summarized by Sky News in January 2017 –

> America is fundamentally a technological nation. Its leaders have always seized upon new tools to further political goals.
>
> The printing press let Ben Franklin distribute pamphlets and kick off a revolution. Lincoln pioneered the telegraph.
>
> In 1897, William McKinley made the first campaign film; he also filmed his inauguration.
>
> Franklin D Roosevelt invited the nation into the White House for intimate, fireside chats delivered by radio.
>
> And although previous presidents had experimented with television, it was JFK who became the first TV president.
>
> Christian Fuchs, professor of social media at Westminster University, told Sky News: "If you look at the evolution of politics, then it stands in relationship to the evolution of technology. Even when politicians and presidents have a lot of attention in public, they try to use the newest technologies. What Trump is using is two media of his time. One is social media, where superficiality, speed and brevity fits his personality. The other one is reality TV". [13]

## 1.6  Conclusions

The origin and historical development of digital media have been reviewed. The visionary concepts and ideas of Vannevar Bush in 1945 have been shown to have been fulfilled at least in part by the developments in hyperlinks in the World Wide Web, digital repositories and encyclopedias, and new ways of working together. The power and capability of processing, storage and network connectivity has facilitated and enabled the development and operation of digital media. This in turn has transformed a wide variety of traditional application areas with significant consequent social and cultural impacts. The advantages and challenges of digital media have been set out and reviewed.

## Further Reading

Barnet, B.: Memory machines: the evolution of hypertext. pp. 192, Anthem Press, London (2013)

Earnshaw, R.A.: Digital media. IEEE Comput. Graphics Appl. IEEE Comput. Soc. **21**(1), 14–17 (2001) http://ieeexplore.ieee.org/xpl/tocresult.jsp?reload=true&isnumber=19362; https://pdfs.semanticscholar.org/f076/2d677686bc37786338bf5e303a8f0b782171.pdf

Logan R. K.: Understanding new media: extending Marshall McLuhan. pp. 389. Peter Lang Publishing Inc, Bern (2010)

McLuhan, M.: Understanding media: extensions of man. New American Library, New York (1964)

Samoff, T.: The history of digital media – from its inception to today. (2016) https://prezi.com/lhgi1fwmb4k2/the-history-of-digital-media/

Tanaka, S.: Digital media in history: remediating data and narratives. (2009). https://www.historians.org/publications-and-directories/perspectives-on-history/may-2009/intersections-history-and-new-media/digital-media-in-history

## References

1. Transcript-Big Think Interview with Nicholas Negroponte. http://talke.ng/transcript-big-think-interview-with-nicholas-negroponte/; http://www.azquotes.com/author/10712-Nicholas_Negroponte (2014)

2. Moore, Gordon E.: Cramming more components onto integrated circuits. Electronics Magazine, p. 4. http://web.eng.fiu.edu/npala/eee6397ex/gordon_moore_1965_article.pdf (1965)

3. Excerpts from A Conversation with Gordon Moore: Moore's Law. Intel Corporation, p. 1. http://large.stanford.edu/courses/2012/ph250/lee1/docs/Excepts_A_Conversation_with_Gordon_Moore.pdf (2005)

4. Bush, V.: As we may think. Atlantic Monthly. http://www.theatlantic.com/magazine/archive/1945/07/as-we-may-think/303881/ (July 1945)

5. Nelson, T.: Computer lib, the dream machine. http://www.newmediareader.com/book_samples/nmr-21-nelson.pdf; https://stummkonzert.de/wp-content/uploads/2012/12/Ted%20Nelson%20-%20Computer%20Lib%20-%20Dream%20Machine.pdf; https://en.wikipedia.org/wiki/Computer_Lib/Dream_Machines (1974)

6. Nelson, T.: Living the dreams: a conversation with Ted Nelson. YouTube. https://www.youtube.com/watch?v=GuU-Urb9AOQ

7. Nelson, T.: Rethink and arise. YouTube. https://www.youtube.com/watch?v=lNAPEPqQjJo

8. Simpson, R., Renear, A., Elli Mylonas, E., van Dam, A.: 50 years after 'As We May Think': the Brown/MIT Vannevar Bush symposium. ACM Interactions, pp. 47–67 (March 1996). "50 years after 'As We May Think': the Brown/MIT Vannevar Bushs ymposium" (PDF)

9. Mynatt, E.: As we may think: the legacy of computing research and the power of human cognition. Computing Research Association. http://archive2.cra.org/ccc/events/past-events/309-as-we-may-think-the-legacy-of-computing-research-and-the-power-of-human-cognition; https://www.youtube.com/watch?v=xouhu5n5sq0

10. https://prezi.com/0aa0y1gpbe8v/the-advantages-of-using-digital-media-over-more-traditional/; https://www.hausmanmarketingletter.com/click-traditional-media-versus-digital-media-versus-social-media/; http://www.hausmanmarketingletter.com/16-differences-between-social-media-and-traditional-media/

11. Crawford, S.P.: Internet access and the new digital divide. New York Times. http://www.nytimes.com/2011/12/04/opinion/sunday/internet-access-and-the-new-divide.html?pagewanted=all&_r=0 (3 December 2011)

12. https://en.wikipedia.org/wiki/One_Laptop_per_Child; http://one.laptop.org/; http://www.olpcnews.com/about_olpc_news/goodbye_one_laptop_per_child.html

13. Cheshire, T.: JFK found a new way to communicate – now Donald Trump has too. Sky News. http://news.sky.com/story/jfk-found-a-new-way-to-communicate-now-donald-trump-has--too-10738000 (21 January 2017)

# Chapter 2
# Key Historical Visions for the Future of Computing and Digital Media

**Abstract** From the earliest days of the development of computers there is clear evidence of visionary thinking that went far beyond the current capability. These developments and this visionary thinking are identified and summarized. In turn, hardware, software, interfaces, and applications have been revolutionized from the earliest days of computing to today. At the same time, a number of the transitions did not appear to develop seamlessly from one to the next but were constrained by a number of cultural or organizational factors. Developments in computing and digital media are not solely determined by the latest advances in technology.

**Keywords** Hyperlinks • World wide web • Digital repositories • Transformative effects • Online collaboration • Higher level tools • Client-server computing • Personal computer • Networked computers • Interactive displays • Desktop computing • Information access • Information search

## 2.1 Introduction

The following historical transitions in the development of computers may be identified. This also affected the way computers were accessed and used, and the range of applications that were considered appropriate to be addressed at the time.

- The switch from electromechanical to electronic devices – leading to the first fully electronic digital computer in the 1940s
- The development of programming languages (1950s)
- Time-sharing (1960s)
- Personal computing (1970s)
- Graphical user interfaces (1980s)
- World wide web (1990s)
- Diversification of access and use (e.g. Internet of Things) (2000s)

It has been argued that these developments were not just technical ones [1–3]. All technologies embody to some degree the physical, intellectual and symbolic resources of the societies that construct them. Thus there appear to have been both

© The Author(s) 2017
R. Earnshaw, *State of the Art in Digital Media and Applications*, SpringerBriefs in Computer Science, DOI 10.1007/978-3-319-61409-0_2

enabling and constricting forces at work in the development pathways of computing. These also included organizational and societal factors such as –

- Support of current practices or traditions in computer designs
- Favoring particular kinds of interpersonal relationships
- Looking to particular visionaries and leaders
- Considering complex cultural aspects [1]

This may help to explain some of the enigmas that appear to characterize the
development of computing and its uses such as –

- Relatively slow development of high-level languages
- Continuing with mainframe computing when client-server computing offered
  more flexibility
- Underestimating the significance of the development of the personal computer
- Insufficient attention being paid to graphical user interfaces

However, the development pathway was characterized by a number of key
visions that have been both significant and lasting, and these are reviewed in this
chapter. Some of them also have implications for the future of computing and digital
media because they may not have been fully realized or achieved.

## 2.2   What Could a Computer Do?

In 1945, Vannevar Bush stated –.

> Consider a future device for individual use, which is a sort of mechanized private file and
> library. It needs a name, and, to coin one at random, 'memex' will do. A memex is a device
> in which an individual stores all his books, records, and communications, and which is
> mechanized so that it may be consulted with exceeding speed and flexibility. It is an enlarged
> intimate supplement to his memory [4].

As set out in Chap. 1, Sect. 1.4 Origins of Digital Media –

> Although the memex was never created, it was nevertheless very far sighted. This concep-
> tual system of devices contains early intimations of the links between relevant items of
> information (such as was eventually realized as hyperlinks in the World Wide Web); digital
> repositories and encyclopaedias (such as was eventually implemented by Wikipedia); and
> new ways of working together resulting in human insight, discovery, and scholarship (such
> as was eventually implemented in email and social media). It is clear that all these elements
> have had a significant transformative effect on the digital environment and how it is cre-
> ated, accessed, and used. Various papers and conferences have analysed the extent to which
> these early ideas have facilitated development and progress [5–9].

### Key Points of the Vision

- Hyperlinks in the World Wide Web enable hierarchical documents to be created
  with links to other documents containing more information
- Online books and digital repositories are directly accessible to users and readers
  over the Internet

- New ways of collaborating online using email, shared documents, and social media resulting in greater and quicker human insight, discovery, and scholarship than working with paper documents alone

## 2.3   Higher Level Interfaces to Computers

In 1949 Grace Hopper believed a wider audience would be able to use the computer provided higher level tools were available that could be used by coders and programmers, and which were also closer to the functions and terms used in the application (i.e. user and application-friendly) rather than being closer to the assembly language required by the machine. This required an appropriate system (called a compiler) to convert the higher level program into the equivalent low level assembly program which was then run on the computer. This concept led to the development of Cobol in 1959, the first business-oriented programming language [10].

**Key Points of the Vision**

- Computers need to be easy to program, i.e. sufficiently high level
- The programming interface needs to be suitable for the application area, i.e. application-friendly

## 2.4   The Rate of Growth of Computer Power

Moore's law states that overall processing power for computers doubles every 1.5–2 years, or less [11]. This also applies to telecommunications. Although a general guide rather than a fundamental law, it has proved remarkably consistent since the implementation of the first semiconductor integrated circuit in 1960.

**Key Points of the Vision**

- Computer power, memory, and telecommunications speeds are expected to do double every 1.5–2 years. Therefore over time, sufficient power would be available for more sophisticated and compute-intensive applications
- For more advanced applications and requirements, general users and home users can access supercomputer power in the cloud when they need it [12]

## 2.5   The Networked Computer

Licklider, Vice President at Bolt Beranek and Newman, Inc., proposed a global network in his January 1960 paper Man-Computer Symbiosis [13].

*A network of such [computers], connected to one another by wide-band communication lines [which provided] the functions of present-day libraries together with anticipated advances in information storage and retrieval and [other] symbiotic functions.*

**Key Points of the Vision**

• Network of digital functions to implement a digital library

## 2.6   The Interactive Computer

More general forms of interaction were accomplished by interactive displays from 1963 (e.g. Sketchpad [14]). However, varying the shape and size of letters on the screen was limited with vector displays.

*The screen is a window through which one sees a virtual world. The challenge is to make that world look real, act real, sound real, feel real* [15].

It was not until the first bit-mapped screen in the Xerox Alto (in 1981), followed by others, and the Apple Macintosh in 1984 (72 pixels per inch) that desktop publishing became possible.

**Key Points of the Vision**

• The screen is key – whether for viewing or interaction
• The window of the screen gives the viewer direct access to the model displayed in the virtual world in the computer
• The bit-mapped screen (at 72 pixels per inch) initiated desktop publishing because it provided higher quality typography and character generation for documents than was possible on the typical alphanumeric display

## 2.7   The Personal Computer

Bill Gates's dream in 1980 was *"a computer on every desk and in every home"* [16]. Microsoft grew to 80,000 employees in over 100 countries. It developed the operating system MS-DOS and the programming language Basic. Microsoft dominated the desktop computing space, and its Windows operating system, which first launched in 1985, is still used on 90 per cent of the world's computers. In 1989, Microsoft consolidated its position with the release of Office, a suite of word processing and database tools that blurred the line between work and play, and turned the home computer into a powerful creative tool.

In 1992 Bill Gates received the National Medal of Technology and Innovation Award for his early vision of universal computing at home and in the office; for his technical and business management skills in creating a worldwide technology company; and for his contribution to the development of the personal computer industry [17].

Historically, graphics designers favored the Macintosh because of its more powerful processors and its graphics community [18]. However, the internal components are now very similar for both Mac and PC. In addition, the application interface to the user for most programs is now the same, so in theory it makes little difference whether the underlying platform is Windows PC or Mac [19, 20]. The latter is normally more expensive than the PC. If more general computing facilities are required (e.g. for business computing) in addition to those for art and design, it may be an advantage to use a Windows PC because of the wider variety of more general software that is available.

**Key Points of the Vision**

- The personal computer and the Mac brought desktop computing to every desk and every home and offered the potential for many forms of computing and applications

## 2.8   The World Wide Web

NSFNET was established in 1986 with 56 kbit/s links and was followed by the World Wide Web in 1991 [21]. The World Wide Web has transformed computing and the connectivity of computers and information, initiated by Sir Tim Berners-Lee.

**Key Points of the Vision**

- The World Wide Web brought connectivity and information to all computers on the Internet

  In 2009, Vincent Cerf, Vice-President of Google, said –.

  *We never, ever in the history of mankind have had access to so much information so quickly and so easily* [22].

**Key Points of the Vision**

- Fast and easy access to information

## 2.9   Digital Content

In 2014, Negroponte stated –.

*When we ship our laptop, we ship 1.6 million books with it. You can access free, 1.6 million books and embedded in the laptop are 100 books per laptop of the choosing of the country, but what's important about that is, when you ship 100 laptops into a village, there are 100 different books on each of the laptops, so the village now has 10,000 books in the village and 1.6 million accessible. That's—that is really, really different.*

*So, to compare books to computers, I mean, computers are the way to get books. That is the medium for distributing text because it doesn't require paper, it doesn't—you know, it's editable. Nothing goes out of date, nothing goes out of print, it can be refreshed and updated* [23].

**Key Points of the Vision**

- Digital content gives unparalleled flexibility in the creation, distribution, storage, and updating of content
- Digital content can provided opportunities for interaction by the user, including searching for particular sections or words

## 2.10   Summary of the Key Historical Visions

Table 2.1 provides a timeline of the Key Visions.

## 2.11   Key Visions Historical and Current Which Are Relevant to Digital Media

A number of the companies in Table 2.1 have products and services relevant to the development of digital media and its applications. Their missions are summarized in Table 2.2.

A number of further current visionaries, organizations, and companies are building on the foundations summarized in this chapter. These are relevant to the ongoing development of digital media and its applications and are included in Table 2.3.

In addition, there is a wide variety of small companies that are engaged in digital media. In particular, creative industries are often driven by Small and Media Enterprises (SMEs). It is possible that small companies and organizations such as these could have a more significant effect on the field and its developments than the larger companies because they can be more agile and seize niche opportunities in real time before they become mainstream. When they develop key technology and/ or attract a large number of users to their services, they can become candidates for acquisition by larger companies – as has happened with a number of the companies in Table 2.3 (this is noted in the left hand column).

There are at least 22 virtual communities each with over 100 million active users [24].

**Table 2.1**  Timeline of the key visions

| Date | Person | Key vision | Area | Degree of impact and success |
|------|--------|-----------|------|------------------------------|
| 1945 | Vannevar Bush (US OSRD) | Personalized memex computer with accessible information | Books, records, and communications | High |
| 1949 | Grace Hopper (Eckert-Mauchly Computer Corp.) | Envisaged wider use of computers | Applications | High |
| 1959 | Grace Hopper (US Navy) | Cobol | Business applications | High |
| 1960 | Gordon Moore (Intel Corp.) | Integrated circuit | Computer power, memory, and telecommunications speeds are expected to do double every 1.5–2 years. | High |
| 1960 | Joseph Licklider (MIT) | Global network | Network of digital functions to implement a digital library | High |
| 1968 | Ivan Sutherland (E & S Computer Corp.) | Interaction | Computer screen and interaction device | High |
| 1980 | Bill Gates (Microsoft) | Personal computer | Computer on every desk and in every home | High |
| 1984 | Steve Jobs (Apple) | Apple Macintosh | Bit-mapped screen | High |
| 1991 | Sir Time Berners-Lee (MIT) | World Wide Web | Connectivity and access to information | High |
| 1994 | David Filo, Jerry Yang (Yahoo) | Information access | To connect people to their passions, communities, and the world's knowledge | High |
| 1997 | Reed Hastings, Marc Randolph (Netflix) | Video via Internet | Streaming media and video-on-demand | High |
| 2009 | Vincent Cerf (Google) | Information access | Fast and easy access to information | High |
| 2010 | Nicholas Negroponte (MIT) | Digital content | Creation, distribution, storage, searching, and updating of content | High |

**Table 2.2** Current visionaries, organizations, and companies

| Company | Founder(s) | Date | Mission | No of employees (approx) |
|---|---|---|---|---|
| Microsoft | Bill Gates, Paul Allen | 1975 | To enable people and businesses throughout the world to realize their full potential | 120,000 |
| | | | https://www.microsoft.com/ | |
| Apple | Steve Jobs, Steve Wozniak, Ronald Wayne | 1976 | Apple designs Macs, the best personal computers in the world, along with OS X, iLife, iWork and professional software. Apple leads the digital music revolution with its iPods and iTunes online store. Apple has reinvented the mobile phone with its revolutionary iPhone and App store, and is defining the future of mobile media and computing devices with iPad. | 222,000 |
| | | | http://www.apple.com/ | |
| Yahoo | David Filo, Jerry Yang | 1995 | To connect people to their passions, communities, and the world's knowledge. | 8500 |
| | | | https://www.yahoo.com/ | |
| Netflix | Reed Hastings, Marc Randolph | 1997 | Streaming media and video-on-demand online and DVD by mail. | 3700 |
| | | | https://www.netflix.com/ | |
| Google | Larry Page, Sergey Brin | 1998 | To organize the world's information and make it universally accessible and useful | 72,000 |
| | | | https://www.google.com/ | |

## 2.12   Conclusions

The key developments in computing of most relevance to digital media have been reviewed and summarized. The key visions associated with these developments have been identified. The inspiration and innovation associated with these developments is immense and has driven the development of technology and its uses to the advanced level everywhere in evidence in society today.

The convergence of IT, telecommunications, and media is currently bringing about a revolution in the way information is collected, stored and accessed. There are three principal reasons why this is happening – reducing cost, increasing quality, and increasing bandwidth.

**Table 2.3** Further current visionaries, organizations, and companies

| Company | Founder(s) | Date | Mission | No of employees (approx.) |
|---|---|---|---|---|
| Baidu | Robin Li, Eric Xu | 2000 | Many services, including a Chinese search engine for websites, audio files and images. Baidu offers 57 search and community services including Baidu Baike (an online, collaboratively built encyclopedia) and a searchable, keyword-based discussion forum. | 43,500 |
| | | | http://www.baidu.com/ | |
| LinkedIn (acquired by Microsoft in 2016 for $26 bn) | Reid Hoffman, Konstantin Guericke, Jean-Luc Vaillant, Allen Blue, Eric Ly | 2002 | Business and employment-oriented social networking service that operates via websites. | 9700 |
| | | | www.linkedin.com | |
| MySpace | Tom Anderson, Chris DeWolfe | 2003 | Social networking website offering an interactive, user-submitted network of friends, personal profiles, blogs, groups, photos, music, and videos. | 200 |
| | | | https://myspace.com/ | |
| Right Media (acquired by Yahoo in 2007 for ~$680 m) | Michael Walrath and brothers, Noah and Jonah Goodhart | 2003 | Operates the Right Media Exchange, a marketplace that enables advertisers, publishers, and ad networks to trade digital media. | Not known |
| | | | http://www.rightmedia.com/ | |
| Facebook | Dustin Moskovitz, Mark Zuckerberg, Andrew McCollum, Eduardo Saverin, Chris Hughes | 2004 | To give people the power to share and make the world more open and connected. | 17,000 |
| | | | http://www.facebook.com/ | |
| Flickr | Ludicorp | 2004 | Image hosting and video hosting website and web services suite that was created by Ludicorp in 2004. An online community, the service is widely used by photo researchers and by bloggers to host images that they embed in blogs and social media. | Not known |
| | | | https://www.flickr.com/ | |

(continued)

**Table 2.3** (continued)

| Company | Founder(s) | Date | Mission | No of employees (approx.) |
|---|---|---|---|---|
| YouTube (acquired by Google in 2006 for ~$1.65 bn) | Chad Hurley, Jawed Karim, Steve Chen | 2005 | To provide fast and easy video access and the ability to share videos frequently<br>https://www.youtube.com/ | 700 |
| Twitter | Jack Dorsey, Noah Glass, Evan Williams, Biz Stone | 2006 | To give everyone the power to create and share ideas and information instantly, without barriers<br>https://twitter.com/ | 3500 |
| Tumblr (acquired by Yahoo in 2013 for ~$1.1 bn) | David Karp | 2007 | *To empower creators to make their best work and get it in front of the audience they deserve. Microblogging and social media networking website.*<br>https://www.tumblr.com/ | 397 |
| Bluefin Labs (acquired by Twitter in 2013 for ~$90 m) | Michael Fleischman, Deb Roy | 2008 | Social TV analytics company that uses publicly available social media commentary from Twitter, Facebook and blogs to measure viewer engagement with television shows and adverts at scale.<br>https://bluefinlabs.com/ | 11–50 |
| Instagram (acquired by Facebook in 2012 for ~$1 bn) | Kevin Systrom, Mike Krieger<br>Kevin Systrom, Mike Krieger | 2010 | Mobile photo-sharing application and service that allows users to share pictures and videos either publicly or privately on the service, as well as through a variety of other social networking platforms, such as Facebook, Twitter, Tumblr, and Flickr.<br>https://www.instagram.com/ | Not known |
| Periscope (acquired by Twitter before launch in 2015 for ~$50 m) | Kayvon Beykpour, Joe Bernstein | 2015 | Live video streaming app for iOS and Android. Explore the world through the eyes of someone else.<br>https://www.periscope.tv/ | Not known |
| Berne (acquired by CNN in 2016 for ~$25 m) | Casey Neistat https://www.youtube.com/user/caseyneistat | 2015 | Video messaging and social networking. | 11 |

## Further Reading

Berners-Lee, T.: Weaving the Web: The Past, Present, and Future of the World Wide Web by Its Inventor. pp. 256. Texere Publishing, Knutsford (2000)

Beyer, K.W.: Grace Hopper and the Invention of the Information Age. pp. 404. MIT Press, Cambridge (2012)

Isaacson, W.: Steve Jobs: The Exclusive Biography. pp. 592. Abacus, London (2015)

Maeda, J., Negroponte, N.: Maeda@Media, pp. 480, Thames and Hudson, London (2000)

Negroponte, N.: Being Digital. pp. 256. Hodder and Stoughton, London (1995)

Nelson, T.H.: Computer Lib/Dream Machines. http://www.newmediareader.com/book_samples/nmr-21-nelson.pdf; https://en.wikipedia.org/wiki/Computer_Lib/Dream_Machines (1974)

Vince, J.A., Earnshaw, R.A. (eds.): Digital Convergence: The Information Revolution, pp. 350, Springer, London (1999). ISBN: 1-85,233-140-2. http://www.springer.com/gb/book/9781447112204

Waldrop, M.M.: The Dream Machine: J.C.R.Licklider and the Revolution that Made Computing Personal. pp. 512. Penguin Books, London (2002)

## References

1. Tedre, M.: The development of computer science: a sociocultural perspective. Ph.D. Thesis, pp. 502. University of Joensuu, Finland (2006). ftp://cs.joensuu.fi/pub/Dissertations/tedre.pdf
2. Tedre, M., Sutinen, E., Kahkonen, E., Kommers, P.: Ethnocomputing: ICT in cultural and social context. Commun. ACM Pers. Inf. Manag. **49**(1), 126–130 (2006). doi:10.1145/1107458.1107466
3. Tedre, M.: The Science of Computing: Shaping a Discipline, p. 292. Chapman and Hall/CRC, London (2014)
4. Bush, V.: As we may think. The Atlantic Monthly July 1945. https://www.theatlantic.com/magazine/archive/1945/07/as-we-may-think/303881/. Citations from online version available at: http://www.theatlantic.com/unbound/flashbks/computer/bushf.htm
5. Nelson, T.: Computer Lib, The Dream Machine. http://www.newmediareader.com/book_samples/nmr-21-nelson.pdf; https://stummkonzert.de/wp-content/uploads/2012/12/Ted%20Nelson%20-%20Computer%20Lib%20-%20Dream%20Machine.pdf; https://en.wikipedia.org/wiki/Computer_Lib/Dream_Machines (1974)
6. Nelson, T.: Living the dreams: a conversation with Ted Nelson. YouTube. https://www.youtube.com/watch?v=GuU-Urb9AOQ
7. Nelson, T.: Rethink and arise. YouTube. https://www.youtube.com/watch?v=lNAPEPqQjJo
8. Simpson, R., Renear, A., Elli Mylonas, E., van Dam, A.: 50 years after 'As We May Think': the Brown/MIT Vannevar Bush symposium. ACM Interactions, pp. 47–67, March 1996. "50 years after 'As We May Think': the Brown/MIT Vannevar Bush symposium" (PDF).
9. Mynatt, E.: As we may think: the legacy of computing research and the power of human cognition. Computing Research Association. http://archive2.cra.org/ccc/events/past-events/309-as-we-may-think-the-legacy-of-computing-research-and-the-power-of-human-cognition; https://www.youtube.com/watch?v=xouhu5n5sq0
10. http://www.cs.yale.edu/homes/tap/Files/hopper-story.html
11. Moore, G.E.: Cramming more components onto integrated circuits. Electronics Magazine (1965)
12. https://www.ibm.com/blogs/cloud-computing/2016/11/bringing-supercomputing-masses/
13. Licklider, J.C.R.: Man-Computer Symbiosis. IRE Transactions on Human Factors in Electronics. HFE-1: 4–11. (1960) doi:10.1109/thfe2.1960.4503259

14. Sutherland, I.E.: Sketchpad: a man-machine graphical communication system. AFIPS '63 (Spring) Proceedings of the conference, 1963, pp. 329–346. http://dl.acm.org/citation.cfm?id=1461591. doi:10.1145/1461551.1461591; https://www.cl.cam.ac.uk/techreports/UCAM-CL-TR-574.pdf (1963)
15. Sutherland, I.E..: http://www.azquotes.com/author/43063-Ivan_Sutherland (1965)
16. http://www.reliableplant.com/Read/2432/power-of-a-clear,-concise-vision; http://www.telegraph.co.uk/technology/3357701/Bill-Gatess-dream-A-computer-in-every-home.html
17. https://www.uspto.gov/learning-and-resources/ip-programs-and-awards/national-medal-technology-and-innovation/recipients/1992
18. http://www.macworld.co.uk/feature/mac/best-mac-for-graphic-design-buying-guide-2016-2017-3450093/
19. https://www.youtube.com/watch?v=0wMZGcWAMxc
20. http://rtmpcrepair.com/apple-mac-vs-windows-pc-for-graphic-artists-design-and-general-users-2015/
21. https://en.wikipedia.org/wiki/History_of_the_Internet; http://www.agocg.ac.uk/reports/mmedia/network1/report/del3.htm; http://www-bcf.usc.edu/~wdutton/comm533/WWW-WANG.htm; https://en.wikipedia.org/wiki/History_of_the_World_Wide_Web
22. Silva, D.: Internet has only just begun, say founders. https://phys.org/news/2009-04-internet-begun-founders.html; http://www.azquotes.com/author/2658-Vinton_Cerf (2009)
23. Transcript-Big Think Interview with Nicholas Negroponte. http://talke.ng/transcript-big-think-interview-with-nicholas-negroponte/;http://www.azquotes.com/author/10712-Nicholas_Negroponte
24. https://en.wikipedia.org/wiki/List_of_virtual_communities_with_more_than_100_million_active_users

# Chapter 3
# Collaboration on Digital Media

**Abstract** The development of products and services in the area of digital media aims to meet current and future user needs and requirements. Such products and services are often dependent on the results of new research and development within the academy and other research and development organizations. Partnership arrangements between these organizations, industry, and appropriate Small and Medium Enterprises (SMEs) can assist in the development of such products and services, and the migration of such developments into wider society. An additional factor in the area of digital media is that there may often be interdisciplinary components to the research and development, and also the product or service that is developed. This is because of the nature of digital media, and the diversity of its constituent parts, and potential uses, such as electronic devices, sensors, software, firmware, digital images, digital audio, digital video, computer games, web pages, data, databases, social media, e-books, and Internet of Things. Digital media has a wide range of application areas and potential uses. Such users can come from a variety of backgrounds and cultures and therefore the products and services need to meet this diversity of requirements and ways of working. This in turn requires effective collaboration across traditional boundaries between disciplines.

**Keywords** Interdisciplinary research • Small and medium enterprises • Collaborative research and development • Team working • Small and medium enterprises

## 3.1 Introduction

*Where do new ideas come from? The answer is simple: differences. While there are many theories of creativity, the only tenet they all share is that creativity comes from unlikely juxtapositions. The best way to maximize differences is to mix ages, cultures, and disciplines.* Nicholas Negroponte [1]

Collaboration in the field of the academy and industry collaboration, and in creative industries, is discussed in Chap. 4 in [2] Collaboration in the field of art and design is discussed in Chap. 3 in [3]. The benefits and challenges are summarized.

© The Author(s) 2017
R. Earnshaw, *State of the Art in Digital Media and Applications*, SpringerBriefs in Computer Science, DOI 10.1007/978-3-319-61409-0_3

Digital media has a wide range of possible components and potential uses. This in turn requires effective collaboration across traditional boundaries between disciplines. An initial discussion of this point is contained in Chap. 3 in [4]. This present chapter discusses the interdisciplinary challenges in more detail. In addition, the ready availability of tools and facilities for digital media provides exciting opportunities for the user as a creator and distributor of digital content.

## 3.2   Creative Collaboration

As noted in [3] a creative collaboration has the goal of generating a product or service. A team may be needed rather than a single individual because of the volume of work, the input required from different disciplines, or because the multifaceted nature of the task requires multiple skills.

According to Cox [5], it is necessary to consider some codes of behavior for successful teams to be able to work successfully –

1. *There must be a common, passionate goal for the team members*
2. *Members must have mutual respect for each other member and his/her discipline*
3. *Each member must be willing to learn from other members of the team*
4. *Each member must recognize other's intellectual territory*
5. *The team should not have too many members*
6. *The team must continually check to make sure that the research is making progress*
7. *Members must not become over-committed to other projects*
8. *One person must carry the flag for project as a champion and coordinate efforts*
9. *Each member must be credited and given his/her recognition when the project is presented or publicized*
10. *Each member must get something out of the project which is personally rewarding and tangible* [5]

## 3.3   Antidisciplinary Research

The MIT Media Laboratory is an antidisciplinary research laboratory working to invent the future [6]. Antidisciplinary implies beyond existing disciplines and a field of study with its own vocabulary, methods and strategies [7].

## 3.4   Advantages and Difficulties of Interdisciplinary Research and Development

Partnership and collaboration between researchers and industry can often facilitate the development of new products and services in the area of digital media. Such collaborations often cut across traditional disciplines, or require expertise from more than one discipline.

The advantages and difficulties of interdisciplinary research and development are now summarized.

### 3.4.1   Advantages

(i)  Growth at the Boundaries of Existing Disciplines

New disciplines often grow at the boundaries of existing ones, e.g. genetic engineering (genetics/biotechnology), tribology (mechanical engineering/materials science), digital media (computer science/media/application domains), to name but a few. Such new areas offer researchers tremendous opportunities to advance the frontiers of knowledge for the benefit of society, industry, and the academy [8, 9, 10].

(ii)  Potential for Knowledge Transfer to Industry and Society

New disciplines can present exciting opportunities for those involved at the ground level. There can also be significant potential in some areas for the generation of intellectual property that industry can translate into new and novel products and services that can be utilized by society. To continue the examples in the previous section, this could be illustrated by genetic engineering – with genetically modified crops – with greater resistance to disease; in tribology – with artificial joints; and in digital media – with social media. All these areas have made a significant impact on society with their products and services.

(iii)  Freedom and Opportunity

New discipline areas appear to be flatter in their structures and organization and less subject to domination by hierarchies of senior faculty with strong views about what research should be done. Thus there can be more freedom, flexibility, and opportunity in new and emerging discipline areas. It provides time for the new discipline area to define a structure and organization most appropriate for moving it forward.

(iv)  Publication

Generally there are more opportunities for publication of interdisciplinary research in conferences and journals because the work will done will often be both new and novel. The downside to this is that it will probably be difficult to get acceptance in a world-leading journal (e.g. IEEE or ACM Transactions) as these cater for traditional discipline areas that have been well-established over a period of many years They are also very discipline specific, and with many paper submissions. This emphasizes the strategic importance of having a leading author of the paper who is highly regarded and working in a well-regarded center of excellence. Whether or not this is possible, it may still be necessary to begin publication in a journal of lower standing and work up to the higher levels if possible. The problem in this area is compounded in the UK because the periodic research audit exercise (REF) now only leads to funding for research (the QR component[Ref to book 1]) that is classed as world-leading (4*) and internationally excellent (3*). As 60% of this grading is determined by the quality of the published work submitted to the audit, there is clearly a significant drive to ensure that the publications of all faculty in the UK appear in the highest quality vehicles with clear international standing and reputation (and therefore known to be the most rigorous and selective in their international refereeing processes) in order to increase the possibility of a high grading in the REF review process. Thus there is now increased competition for publication in the highest quality international journals and conferences [11], even though the review process in the REF concentrates solely on the content within the paper and not its publication vehicle, nor its impact factor. However, the citation data for papers was made available to the REF reviewers. Clearly papers published in world-leading journals tend on average to be the most important papers in the field and therefore stand a greater chance of more citations, because more researchers will be looking at them [12].

(v) Lines of Reporting

Some new areas have been able to move their initiative out of the initial academic department or faculty (with its associated department head or chair to which reporting was made) into a university research center where the head of the new area reported directly to the provost or vice-president of the university. This resolves the potential issue of tensions within the department about the new area but brings substantial responsibilities for the new center to bring in substantial grant or sponsorship funding to support all its staff, researchers, equipment, and overheads. The new area is no longer able to rely on the overarching department to defray some of the infrastructure costs in its general budget. Generally such initiatives will not be approved unless the provost or vice-president is convinced by the business plan of the head of the new area that they will be able to generate revenue to fully support the work of the new center to enable it to operate independently. It will then be able to make its own collaborations with other academic areas or other institutions (and possible have funding to also support them) to further develop its work. An example of this is the Scientific Computing and Imaging Institute at the University of Utah [13, pp. 74–76]

## 3.4.2   Disadvantages

(i)  Interdisciplinary Journals and Conferences

Interdisciplinary journals and conferences are relatively new, are not yet well-established, and therefore tend to have a relatively low impact factor, H-index, and citation levels of papers. These may become a significant aspect for the reputational value of the research reported and could affect promotion prospects, tenure prospects, and the general perception of the standing of the particular research area and its potential to attract future grant funding, and also good researchers to work in it. It can be difficult therefore to get published and establish a peer reviewed track record in a multidisciplinary area [14].

(ii)  Applications to Grant Awarding Bodies and Agencies

Grant proposals are often reviewed by subject experts in the different disciplines contained in the proposal (often described as cross-referral), rather than interdisciplinary experts in the particular disciplines. This is because the procedures for selection and appointment of reviewers within grant awarding bodies is normally based upon performance and achievement within the existing disciplines – often to world or international standards, so the disciplines need to be well-established. This can lead to rejection if the subject expert ranks the subject component in the proposal as of less merit than that expected in a grant proposal that is solely within the subject area of the expert. In other words, the added value from one discipline to another may not be fully recognized or evaluated. In many interdisciplinary research proposals, the whole can be significantly greater than the sum of the parts. This may be very difficult to evaluate in an emerging area. In addition, evaluators may be unsure whether the proposers are leaders in their fields or not, and also whether the work is innovative or not.

(iii)  Culture and Working Practices in Different Disciplines

Culture, vocabulary, and working practice differences in different disciplines may be initially difficult for junior researchers to accommodate in team working (and older researchers too!).

(iv)  Relationship to Senior Faculty and the University

High achieving faculty in well-established disciplines can be overly dismissive of new emerging disciplines and may regard them as 'applications', 'not academic', and 'lightweight'. It is recognized that such terms were sometimes used of computing when it emerged as a new discipline in the 1950s.

Chapter 2 has demonstrated that when computing technology was first developed it was not clear to many of those involved how far-reaching these developments would become, nor precisely what form these would take. This has also been repeated at key points during the subsequent development of computing technology. It has been hard to predict, but easy to be wise with the benefit of hindsight.

Similarly, it can take a significant amount of time to establish a new discipline in a university as it is in competition for resources with well-established disciplines and most of these tend to be very reluctant to see part of their own budget, or their space allocation, go to a new area. Indeed, there are still some areas within computer science that are still regarded in the same way that computer science was regarded as a whole. It can also generate tensions and misunderstandings between senior and junior faculty and their researchers. Senior faculty have generally progressed up the hierarchy in academia when the demarcation lines between different disciplines were very clearly defined. However, computing was fortunate. When the first computers were operational they rapidly became important national initiatives in many countries, and the universities received major grants from their national governments to establish their computing facilities, relatively primitive though they were at the time. These were immediately utilized by faculty and research students who could see the significant potential for their work (this latter point could also be regarded as a 'Pro' because such facilities opened up new avenues and new results that would otherwise not have been possible using the existing approaches in the traditional disciplines). Access to computing power constituted a major step change in the management, operation, and delivery of research results in many, if not all, disciplines. However, this did not stop some academic critics still referring to computer science as "merely applications of computing" with insufficient academic merit to be considered an academic discipline in its own right. Although this argument has essentially been won for computer science as a whole, the same argument is still being used within computer science by those that consider that their area is more meritorious than others. External observers of this have expressed the view that computer science has generally failed to learn the lesson that that the physical sciences have learned, viz, to present a united front to the outside world and not let vocal internal disagreements about priorities within the area devalue grant bids and requests to governments for budgets.

(v)  Tenure Committee Considerations

New discipline areas can cause difficulties with tenure awarding committees in the academy because the application of traditional criteria may not be fully appropriate. There may also be additional concerns (whether real or not) about the long term viability of the new area, and therefore its ability to earn sufficient revenue to support a tenured faculty member. Such considerations rarely arise in the context of well-established disciplines because the amount they have earned over the years is fully documented and clear extrapolations can be made about the future. Thus involvement in interdisciplinary areas can affect the career advancement and tenure decisions for faculty who research in these particular areas [15].

(vi)  Employment of Faculty on Part-Time or Zero-Hours Contracts

Many universities are limiting their financial commitments by employing faculty on part-time or zero hours contracts. In the UK, when the use of typical academic staff is factored in, 54% of all academic staff and 49% of all academic teaching staff are on insecure contracts [UCU data]. This means that these faculty are in working conditions that leave them poorly paid, vulnerable, and constantly facing the prospect of unemployment [16].

In the USA, 76% of academics are in casual nonpermanent posts (with 70% of these being part-time), according to the American Federation of Teachers (AFT), the largest Higher Education union. Many teach at a number of institutions to generate income – and have to travel between these institutions at their own expense. The AFT calculates that the median pay per course per semester for such staff is around $2700, meaning that an experienced professional teaching three courses a semester might earn only $24,300 a year [17].

The implications of this trend is that the number of advertised tenure track positions is relatively low, so the chances of a tenured career in academia are slim, and are likely to be available to only the very highest performers in traditional disciplines. New disciplines are likely to be an even lower priority for tenured posts. The key primary driver is now economic, not developing new disciplines.

## 3.5  Conclusions

Effective collaboration has the power to add significant value to digital media research and development and the products and services that are the outcomes. Such collaboration is not without its challenges and difficulties, particularly in the area of enabling collaboration across the boundaries and ways of working associated with traditional disciplines. However, a changing world requires changing ways of working in order to be effective.

## Further Reading

Catmull, E.: Creativity, Inc.: Overcoming the Unseen Forces That Stand in the Way of True Inspiration. pp. 368, Bantam Press, London (2014).
Lowgren, J., Reimer, B.: Collaborative Media: Production, Consumption, and Design Interventions. pp. 208, MIT Press, Cambridge (2013)
Thomas K., Chan J. (Eds): Handbook of Research on Creativity. pp. 584. Edward Elgar Publications, Cheltenham (2015)

## References

1. http://www.azquotes.com/author/10712-Nicholas_Negroponte
2. Earnshaw, R.A.: Research and Development in the Academy, Creative Industries and Applications. Springer, Cham (2017a)
3. Earnshaw, R.A.: Art, Design and Technology: Collaboration and Implementation. Springer, Cham (2017b)

4. Earnshaw, R.A.: Research and Development in Art, Design and Creativity. Springer, Cham (2017c)
5. http://swiki.cs.colorado.edu/CreativeIT/248.print
6. https://www.media.mit.edu/research/?filter=groups
7. https://joi.ito.com/weblog/2014/10/02/antidisciplinar.html http://opentranscripts.org/transcript/challenging-audience-antidisciplinary-spaces/
8. Blackwell, A.F., Wilson, L., Street, A., Boulton, C., Knell, J.: Radical innovation: crossing knowledge boundaries with interdisciplinary teams, University of Cambridge Computer Laboratory, Cambridge, UK, Technical Report 760, pp. 124. https://www.cl.cam.ac.uk/techreports/UCAM-CL-TR-760.pdf (2009)
9. Krishnan A.: What are Academic Disciplines? Some observations of the Disciplinarity vs Interdisciplinarity Debate, ESRC National Centre for Research Methods, NCRM Working Paper Series, pp. 59. http://www.forschungsnetzwerk.at/downloadpub/what_are_academic_disciplines2009.pdf (2009)
10. Blackwell, A.F., Wilson, L., Boulton, C., Knell, J.: Creating Value across Boundaries: Maximizing the return from Interdisciplinary Innovation, NESTA Research Report, pp. 31. https://www.nesta.org.uk/sites/default/files/creating_value_across_boundaries.pdf (May 2010)
11. Earnshaw, R.A.: Research and Development in Art, Design and Creativity, Springer, pp. 87, Sections 3.1 (pp. 32–33), 5.2.5 (pp. 74–75). ISBN 978-3-319-33005-1 http://dx.doi.org/10.1007/978-3-319-33005-1, http://www.springer.com/gb/book/9783319330044 (2016)
12. http://www.ref.ac.uk/about/guidance/citationdata/; http://www.ref.ac.uk/about/guidance/citationdata/googlescholar/; http://www.ref.ac.uk/pubs/2012-01/#d.en.69569
13. Shneiderman, B.: The New ABCs of Research: Achieving Breakthrough Collaborations, pp. 336. Oxford University Press, Oxford (2016). ISBN 9780198758839
14. Goldin, I., Kutarna, C.: Age of Discovery: Navigating the Risks and Rewards of the New Renaissance, pp. 272. Bloomsbury Information Ltd, London (2016). ISBN-13: 978-1472936370
15. https://www.timeshighereducation.com/news/multidisciplinary-research-career-suicide-junior-academics; https://www.timeshighereducation.com/news/multidisciplinary-study-gets-lip-service-not-cash/420266.article
16. https://www.ucu.org.uk/media/7995/Precarious-work-in-higher-education-a-snapshot-of-insecure-contracts-and-institutional-attitudes-Apr-16/pdf/ucu_precariouscontract_hereport_apr16.pdf; https://www.timeshighereducation.com/news/universities-most-reliant-on-teaching-only-staff-named https://www.timeshighereducation.com/content/few-crumbs-of-comfort-in-a-temporary-lecturers-day; https://www.theguardian.com/commentisfree/2016/nov/17/universities-casual-contracts-casualised-work-profit-academia-staff-students; https://www.theguardian.com/uk-news/2016/nov/16/universities-accused-of-importing-sports-direct-model-for-lecturers-pay; https://www.pressreader.com/uk/the-guardian/20161117/281492160902486; https://www.pressreader.com/uk/the-guardian/20161117/281681139463510
17. http://www.academica.ca/blog/part-time-faculty-what-we-know-and-what-we-dont; http://www.chronicle.com/blogs/conversation/2015/05/12/an-adjuncts-farewell/; https://www.aaup.org/issues/contingency/background-facts; https://www.theguardian.com/education/2015/nov/17/university-lecturers-uk-us-casual-posts-food-stamps https://www.theguardian.com/higher-education-network/2016/feb/12/casual-contracts-are-ruining-universities-for-staff-and-students; http://education.stateuniversity.com/pages/1969/Faculty-Members-Part-Time.html

# Chapter 4
# Digital Imaging

**Abstract** From the earliest days of photography in the 1820s, the still image has been used to record and preserve scenes and events for posterity. The use of photographic film involved elements of photochemical processing to develop and stabilize images. The development of digital cameras in the late 1990s was one of the most significant transitions from traditional processes to ones which were often entirely digital. This was faster, cheaper, and more accurate than chemical processing, and also allowed significant opportunities for subsequent image editing, manipulation, or other forms of processing. This gave the photographer much greater flexibility in the production of final images. It changed the traditional photographic industry completely. It also raised the interesting and relevant question of the meaning of the final image, if it represented some form of advancement from the initial image of the person or scene that was initially photographed. The subsequent development of relatively low-cost mobile phones with integrated cameras and increasing capability in terms of function and resolution provided a further platform for the expansion of low-cost digital imaging. They enabled the recording and storage of both still and video images. Smart phones enable such images to be immediately shared across the Internet using photo-sharing and social web sites. The motion picture industry has also been transformed by the utilization of digital technology. It has enabled more efficient and cheaper copying, distribution, and projection processes for main stream movies, as well as allowing the direct addition of digital special effects during movie post-production. At the same time, digital technology has continued its onward march. Streaming media allows digital content to be downloaded via the Internet, giving more flexibility for the viewer, and challenging traditional distribution mechanisms. Variants on the traditional digital camera have been developed, such as the light-field camera, which captures the intensity of light in a scene and the direction of the light rays. It has the capability to change the focal distance and depth of field after a photograph is taken. Although photography remains a significant art form, and there are many exhibitions which display the work of famous photographers (including those who use modern digital technology as part of their work), todays smart phones have also made photographs more ubiquitous and transitory and many have become an integral part of the social media landscape. Photography and imaging has to a significant extent been redefined from its origins. However, digital media has raised ongoing issues such as copyright, digital media rights, and fair use which are proving difficult to resolve.

© The Author(s) 2017                                                                                     29
R. Earnshaw, *State of the Art in Digital Media and Applications*, SpringerBriefs
in Computer Science, DOI 10.1007/978-3-319-61409-0_4

**Keywords** Analog to digital • Imaging spectrum • Digital processing • sVideo • HDMI • Image manipulation • Light-field • Plenoptic camera • Panoramic photographs • 3D models • Archival images • Photo-sharing • Motion pictures • Special effects • Visual effects • Streaming media • Digital photography

## 4.1   History and Introduction

The rise of 2D digital imaging marked one of the biggest transitions from conventional analog to digital information. The analog process involved elements of chemical and mechanical processing that had become well-established following the earliest photographs in the 1820s. In the 1990s, affordable computer-based digital cameras gave an instantaneous image, and essentially eliminated both delay and cost in the production of images. The knock on effect on traditional film companies such as Kodak, Agfa, and Fuji was dramatic and resulted in their withdrawal from the manufacture and sale of cameras and film. In 2012, Kodak filed for bankruptcy [1]. The reducing cost of mobile phones and the incorporation of digital cameras within the phone has resulted in digital imaging becoming ubiquitous. Smart phones enable such images to be immediately shared across the Internet using photo-sharing sites and social web sites. If a photograph was originally a framing exercise (in the sense of what to include in the picture and what to exclude) it could be argued that it is now more of a social phenomenon. When a camera took time to set up and record an image, more consideration was paid to composition and what the photograph was intended to preserve and communicate [2]. Today's digital cameras and phones are essentially "point and shoot" and are often advertised as such. The word "selfie" has also entered the vocabulary, latterly becoming popular in describing a self-photograph normally taken with a smart digital camera on a stick to give the camera a wider field of view [3]. Selfies are frequently shared on social media sites such as Facebook, Instagram and Twitter, as it is normally easy to do this from a digital camera with an Internet connection. Technology for digital cameras has continued to advance in terms of increasing capability in terms of function and resolution, such as dealing with motion blur, red-eye effects, anti-aliaising, better color, better low-light (or even no light) performance, better facial recognition, etc. [4].

3D models can be created from a collection of 2D images using a variety of software [5]. The resulting scene can be viewed from a number of viewpoints. This is particularly useful for archaeological sites where it is important to keep a record of a site before further excavation is done [6].

Some 3D stereo digital cameras can take 3D panoramic photographs with two lenses, or even a single lens. A digital camera normally has an output port which is normally sVideo, which can be displayed on a television. In addition, HDMI is used on many high end digital cameras for high resolution display on HDTV.

A light-field camera (or plenoptic camera) captures the intensity of light in a scene and their direction. A normal camera only records light intensity [7]. It has the capability of changing the focal distance and depth of field after a photo is taken. Lytro is one company with a light-field camera and was founded by Stanford University Computer Graphics Laboratory alumnus Ren Ng [8].

## 4.2   The Imaging Spectrum

Digital imaging can be conveniently summarized by noting the wavelength of the radiation involved in generating the image.

The electromagnetic spectrum may be divided by wavelength into radio wave, microwave, terahertz radiation, infrared, the visible region (i.e. light), ultraviolet, X-rays and gamma rays as shown in Fig. 4.1. The physical properties of a particular section of electromagnetic radiation depends on the wavelength.

A timeline of imaging technology may be found in [9].

Types of digital imaging used in medical imaging include –

* Digital X-ray imaging
* Digital gamma ray imaging
* Ultrasonography

Medical ultrasound (or ultrasonography) can be used to view sonic images of internal body structures. Gamma cameras detect the radiation from a radioactive source inserted into the patient. Magnetic resonance imaging (MRI) uses magnetic fields, radio waves, and field gradients to generate a picture of the inside of the body using nuclear magnetic resonance [10]. MRI with STIR sequences can be used to produce more information by suppressing the signal from fat. A CAT scan is defined as Computerized Axial Tomography and the associated calculation converts multiple 2D projections (similar to standard X-rays) into 3D images.

## 4.3   Digital Imaging

Digital photography uses visible light to produce images. The advantages of a digital image is that it can be subsequently edited, modified, transformed, or processed with a variety of algorithms (e.g. to modify the lighting, as in Fig. 4.2, or provide special effects in the image).

JPEG is a common method of lossy compression for digital images, particularly for those images produced by digital photography. The degree of compression can be varied, allowing a trade-off between storage size and image quality (Fig. 4.3). JPEG can achieve 10:1 compression with little perceptible loss in image quality.

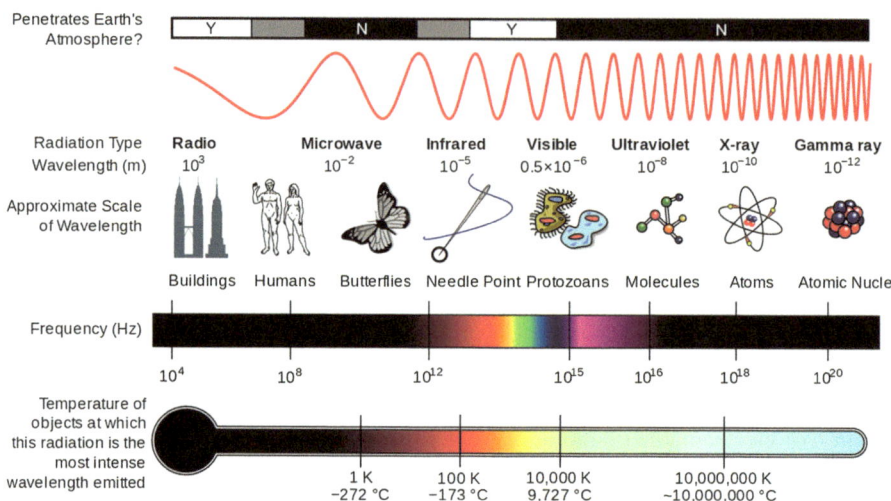

**Fig. 4.1** A diagram of the electromagnetic spectrum, showing various properties across the range of frequencies and wavelengths
(Fig. 4.1 is courtesy of By Inductiveload, NASA – self-made, information by NASABased off of File:EM_Spectrum3-new.jpg by NASA. The butterfly icon is from the P icon set, P biology.svg The humans are from the Pioneer plaque, Human.svg The buildings are the Petronas towers and the Empire State Buildings, both from Skyscrapercompare.svg, CC BY-SA 3.0, https://commons.wikimedia.org/w/index.php?curid=2974242)

**Fig. 4.2** Digital image of the Golden Gate Bridge, San Francisco, modified by light effects
Courtesy of 'By David Ball – Original work', CC BY 2.5, https://commons.wikimedia.org/w/index.php?curid=1536881

## 4.4  The Motion Picture Industry

The issue of "Film versus Digital" has preoccupied the movie industry in recent years [11]. In 2014, Paramount Pictures stated that it would no longer issue 35 mm prints of its movies in the USA. Digital projectors are widely available in larger movie theaters, though the initial investment required ($60K-$150K) may be more difficult to afford for smaller art cinemas. There is little, or no, perceived difference in the movie-viewing experience between film and digital. The cost of shooting a movie in digital format is generally much less than the equivalent recording on film, as is the subsequent post-production and distribution. In addition, a film can be subject to wear and tear over time, whereas the digital version does not degrade. A further aspect to consider is the subsequent distribution of movies after initial release. The sector currently supports distribution of television-based entertainment via companies such as HBO and the streaming of digital video by means of companies such as Netflix and Amazon Prime. It is likely that digital video will gain increasing market share, given the current cost advantages in the use of digital. The precision and reproducibility of the content is also preserved in digital media. Copies can be made that are identical to the original.

Streaming media allows digital content to be downloaded via the Internet, giving more flexibility for the viewer, and challenging more traditional distribution mechanisms. With streaming content, the user does not have to download all the content (whether video, or audio, or both) before viewing it. The service presupposes that the viewer has sufficient bandwidth on their local Internet connection, otherwise they may experience stops and starts in the display of content [12]. Two well-known streaming services are Netflix and YouTube.

The democratization brought about by digital video production, and the ready availability of digital equipment at increasingly low cost, have the potential to decrease the power and influence of large studios and encourage small and independent producers. However, the public still require good quality productions in terms of their content, irrespective of their source and the mechanisms of production. Producing a movie using cheaper and faster methods does not of itself produce a better movie, although it can allow new ideas to enter into the arena and gain visibility and traction. Formerly such new ideas would rarely be considered unless they were backed and financed by a large studio. The key aspect as far as the viewer is concerned is the quality of the content. Of course, new ideas and new videos containing them can be posted in YouTube, and some go viral. This diversity has the potential to allow greater scope for new, creative productions to enter the sector, which is in the overall interests of the consumer.

Therefore the effect of digital media on the move industry has been substantial. It is also an example of how digital media has had a disruptive effect on an area of traditional business and forced it to consider how best to adjust to the new environment, and be able to exist alongside new and exciting developments (Table 4.1).

**Fig. 4.3** Compression rate decreasing, and hence quality increasing, from *left to right*
Courtesy – By Felis_silvestris_silvestris.jpg: Michael Gäblerderivative work: AzaToth – Felis_sil-vestris_silvestris.jpg, CC BY 3.0, https://commons.wikimedia.org/w/index.php?curid=16857750

## 4.5   Archival and Preservation

With regard to archives and preservation, it has been suggested that polyester and chemical film will last for 400–500 years minimum [11]. With regard to digital content, it is not clear how the succession of file formats which characterize the field will affect whether a particular digital format will be readable in a subsequent

**Table 4.1**  A comparison of film and digital methods of movie production

| Point of comparison | Film | Digital |
|---|---|---|
| Start date | 1890s – Lumiere brothers – cinematographe<br>1927 – audio track added | 1990s – affordable digital cameras |
| Precision and reproducibility | Variable | Good |
| Audience viewing | Primarily cinema, though movies available via HBO | Cinemas and home |
| Cost | Typically $1.8 million | $16,000 for 220 h |
| Production and shipping | $1500 to produce and ship a 35 mm film to a cinema.<br>$7.5 million for 5000 prints | 90% less than film |
| Launch of movie | Normally phased across countries | Simultaneously in theaters worldwide and also on digital platforms |
| Wear and tear | Degrades with use | Quality unchanged over time |

Source: https://newrepublic.com/article/119431/how-digital-cinema-took-over-35mm-film

generation, given that often they are not backwards-compatible. This is an issue which affects the archiving and retrieval of digital information as a whole.

## 4.6   Special Effects

Creating artificial dinosaurs for the movie Jurassic Park and making them move realistically and believably is one of the challenges of special effects. Before the widespread use of computer methods, the movie industry relied on physical models which were animated mechanically and with animatronics techniques. It is believed that although Jurassic Park used only 14 min of dinosaur special effects in the final film, of which 4 min were made by computer, it has had a substantial effect on the movie and visual effects industry [13–15]. Such computer sequences can be generated more quickly and cheaply than by conventional means using physical models. They can also be easily modified if the director of the film requires a different effect from that initially planned, in order to fit the story line more effectively.

One example of the functionality and power of visual effects is the movie Toy Story, which was produced 2 years later in 1995 by Pixar, where the entire film consisted of computer-generated animation. Such visual effects are now widespread in the movie industry [16] and they can be so well integrated into the production that it is difficult, if not impossible, to discern where traditional techniques end and the computer-generated sequences begin. In addition, there are now many visual effects companies who use the latest state of the art techniques and are available for hire by production companies.

## 4.7 Special Effects Companies

### 4.7.1 Visual Effects Techniques and Companies

Many special effects companies now use state of the art special effects and animation techniques [17, 18]. A selection is included in Table 4.2.

Data in Table 4.2 is courtesy of [18].

Over 40 Special Effects Companies [18] are listed in Table 4.3 –

The information in Table 4.3 is courtesy of [18].

The next sections summarize how two special effects companies developed, and how they contribute their expertise to visual effects in movies. They are Industrial Light and Magic and Dreamworks. Further information on other companies can easily be found from their company web sites and by reviews of these companies on the Internet.

### 4.7.2 Industrial Light and Magic (ILM)

*Forget the Industrial and Light – this is going to have to be Magic* [19]

ILM can claim to have played a pioneering role in making visual effects for 317 movies [19]. It was founded in 1975 by George Lucas, and was a division of Lucasfilm. In the 1980s and 1990s it developed a reputation for using the latest computer graphics and animation techniques developed for film. It was also the founder company of the animation studio Pixar [20]. In 2012 the Walt Disney Company acquired ILM as part of its purchase of Lucasfilm. ILM has won a number of Oscars for Best Visual Effects, and a number of additional nominations. It has also received a number of Scientific and Technical Awards from the Academy of Motion Picture Arts and Sciences. ILM is one of the largest visual effects companies in the sector with access to one of the largest render farms in the industry [19].

**Table 4.2** A selection of visual special effects techniques

| | | |
|---|---|---|
| Bullet time | Miniature effects | Rotoscoping |
| Computer-generated imagery (often using Shaders) | Morphing | Stop motion |
| | Motion control photography | Go motion |
| Digital compositing | Optical effects | Schüfftan process |
| Dolly zoom | Optical printing | Traveling matte |
| In-camera effects | Practical effects | Virtual cinematography |
| Match moving | Prosthetic makeup effects | Wire removal |
| Matte (filmmaking) and Matte painting | | |

**Table 4.3** A selection of special effects companies

| | | |
|---|---|---|
| Adobe Systems Incorporated (San Jose, CA) | Industrial Light & Magic, founded by George Lucas | Pixomondo (Frankfurt, DE; Munich, DE; Stuttgart, DE; Los Angeles, CA, USA; Beijing, CH; Toronto, ON, CA; Baton Rouge, LA, USA) |
| Animal Logic (Sydney, AU and Venice, CA) | Intelligent Creatures (Toronto, ON, CA) | |
| Bird Studios (London UK) | | |
| BUF Compagnie (Paris, FR) | Intrigue FX (Canada) | Rhythm and Hues Studios (LA, CA, US) |
| CA Scanline (München, DE) | Legacy Effects, (Los Angeles, CA) | Rising Sun Pictures (Adelaide, AU) |
| Cinesite (London/ Hollywood) | Look Effects, (Culver City, CA, USA) | Snowmasters (Lexington, AL, USA) |
| Creature Effects, Inc. (LA, CA, US) | M5 Industries (San Francisco i.e. Mythbusters) | Sony Pictures Imageworks (Culver City, CA, USA) |
| Digital Domain (Venice, LA, CA, US) | Mac Guff (LA, CA, US; Paris, FR) | Strictly FX, live special effects company |
| Double Negative (VFX) (London, UK) | Machine Shop (London, UK) | Surreal World (Melbourne, AU) |
| DreamWorks (LA, CA, US) | Makuta VFX (Universal City, CA) (Hyderabad, India) | Super FX, Special Effects Company, ITALY |
| Flash Film Works (LA, CA, US) | Matte World Digital (Novato, CA) | Tippett Studio (Berkeley, CA, US) |
| Framestore (London, UK) | Method Studios (Los Angeles, CA, USA; New York, NY, USA; Vancouver, BC, CA) | Tsuburaya Productions (Hachimanyama, Setagaya, Tokyo, Jap) |
| Giantsteps (Venice, CA) | | Vision Crew Unlimited |
| Hydraulx (Santa Monica, LA, US) | | |
| Image Engine (Vancouver, BC, CA | The Mill (London, UK; NY and LA, US) | Weta Digital |
| | | Zoic Studios (Culver City, CA, USA) |
| | Modus FX (Montreal, QC, CA) | ZFX Inc a flying effects company |
| | Moving Picture Company (Soho, London, UK) | |
| | Orlando SPFX (Orlando, Fl, US) | |

## *4.7.3 Dreamworks*

DreamWorks was founded in 1994 by Steven Spielberg, Jeffrey Katzenberg and David Geffen. Its objective was to create a new Hollywood studio of which they owned the majority share. DreamWorks used offices at Universal Studios. In

December 2005, the founders agreed to sell the studio to Viacom, parent of Paramount Pictures. The sale was completed in February 2006. In 2008, Dreamworks terminated its partnership with Paramount and signed a $1.5 billion deal to produce films with India's Reliance ADA Group. The following year, DreamWorks entered into an agreement with Walt Disney Studios, with distribution of DreamWorks films through Touchstone Pictures. This continued until 2016. Following the formation of Amblin Partners in 2015, the studio entered into a distribution agreement with Universal Pictures. It has released a number of animated feature films, which include Shrek the Third, Shrek 2 and Madagascar [21].

## 4.8   Image Manipulation Software

### 4.8.1   Commercial Versus Public Domain

An earlier book [22] in Chap. 5 provided a survey of software and applications for the areas of art and design. This section provides a similar analysis for image manipulation software and its application areas.

Commercial software has vendor support and an upgrade path to new versions. However, it has a cost. This may depend upon the version selected – lowest cost versions may contain the smallest number of functions, while the highest cost version contain the most advanced functions.

Public domain software is free and comes without support (though there may be an online community of users who can answer questions by email).

Software is normally available on both Mac and PC. Table 4.4 summarizes a number of commercial applications programs for image manipulation. Table 4.5 summarizes a number of public domain applications programs. Some vendors of commercial software may make earlier versions of their software available as a free download.

**Table 4.4**  Commercial image manipulation software

| Software | Functions | Application areas |
|---|---|---|
| Adobe Photoshop | Enhance photographs, web and mobile app designs, 3D artwork, videos, etc | General |
| ACDSee | Photo editing, photo management | General |
| Sumo Paint | Online image editor | General |
| Aurora HDR | HDR photography software for Mac | Mac |
| ImageMagick | Compose, edit, convert Bitmap images | General |
| Autodesk 3ds Max | 3D modeling and rendering | General |

**Table 4.5**  Free image manipulation software

| Software | Functions | Application areas |
|---|---|---|
| Photobie | Image editing | General |
| Photo!Editor | Image editing | Correct or enhance digital photos |
| Phantasmagoria | Image editing | Enhance digital photos |
| Image Analyzer | Image editing, enhancement and analysis | General |
| Artweaver | Simulates natural brush tools | Brushes |
| Active Pixels | Images | Variety of applications |
| Photoscape | Fix and enhance photos | Photo editing – resize, brightness, color adjustment, etc. |
| VCW VicMan's Photo Editor | Photo editor | General |
| PaintStar | Retouching of photos | General |
| Helicon Filter | Image editing | General |
| Evan's Image Editor | Editing of still or animated images | General |
| Free Image Editor | Bitmap image editor | Digital Photography, print and web |
| Photo Pos Lite | Edit, enhance and manipulate pictures, plus drawing and painting tools | General |
| MAGIX Xtreme Photo Designer | Photo editor | General |
| digiKam | KDE application which acts as a front end to gphoto2 for photo downloads from a digital camera | General |
| Polarr | In-browser photo editor serving pro photographers. It is one of the first photo editors supporting RAW photo editing in web browsers | General |
| Blender | 3D graphics and animation software | General |

Courtesy of – http://www.hongkiat.com/blog/photoshop-alternatives-another-14-free-image-manipulation-tools/; http://www.imaging-resource.com/news/2016/06/18/who-needs-photoshop-the-five-best-free-photo-editing-apps

### 4.8.2   Commercial Image Manipulation Software

Table 4.4 provides a selection of commercial image manipulation software, their functions, and application areas.

### 4.8.3   Public Domain Image Manipulation Software

GNU Image Manipulation Program (GIMP) is a cross-platform image editor available for a variety of platforms including GNU/Linux, OS X, and Windows and more operating systems. It is available free of charge and the source code can be edited.

It is suitable for graphic designers, photographers, illustrators, or scientists. There are also customization options and 3rd party plugins [23].

A variety of public domain image manipulation software is available and some examples are summarized in Table 4.5.

## 4.9  Video Logs

A web log (or blog) is a communication or discussion website [24] normally consisting of short entries of information, or updates to existing information. Such information is normally text and may also contain pictures if they are relevant to the posting. Posts by the author are normally in reverse chronological order so that the most recent information appears first at the top of the page and is therefore easy for users to see when they activate the link to the web site. There are numerous guides on the Internet to starting a blog [25].

A video log (vlog) is a blog where the medium used is video [26] with any associated explanatory text. Vlogs are popular in YouTube [27, 28]. There are numerous guides on the Internet on how to start a vlog [29].

## 4.10  Digital Photography

A digital camera may be freestanding or integrated into a mobile phone. In both cases technology has continued to advance in terms of increasing capability of function and resolution, such as dealing with motion blur, red-eye effects, anti-aliaising, better color, better low-light (or even no light) performance, better facial recognition, etc. [4].

Opinions will vary on the best freestanding digital cameras. This may depend to some degree on the application area in which it is to be used and the preferences of the user with regard to particular functions that are important for their work. One evaluation gave the following 10 best cameras for 2017 [30]. They would all claim to be at the standard required for a professional photographer. Prices shown are in UK pounds sterling (approx.).

1. Fuji X-T2 (£1377)
2. Canon EOS 5D Mark IV (£3499)
3. Nikon D500 (£1729)
4. Sony Alpha A7R II (£999)
5. Nikon D3300 (£319)
6. Panasonic Lumix LX100 (£499)
7. Olympus OM-D E-M10 II (£389)
8. Panasonic Lumix ZS100/TZ100 (£541)
9. Canon EOS Rebel T6i/750D (£488)
10. Panasonic Lumix FZ1000 (£579)

Further information on the specifications of each of the above cameras may be found at [30].

A similar evaluation has been done for the 10 best compact digital cameras for 2017 [31]. Many include Wi-Fi connectivity so photographs can easily be transferred to other people or destinations. Although compact digital cameras tend to be dismissed by professional photographers, there are now many products which offer a competitive alternative to a digital SLR or a mirrorless system camera. In addition, they can also provide an excellent step-up in capability from a smartphone camera where this is required.

Prof Marc Levoy (Google Inc. and Stanford University, USA) gave a series of lectures in 2016 on *"Digital Photography: How cameras work and how to take good pictures using them"* and the lectures were recorded for free public distribution. They are available at a Google URL [32] and also in YouTube [33]. The Course Schedule also contains links to PDFs of the slides used in each lecture [34].

The principal sections of the Lecture Course are as follows –

- Introduction (2 lectures)
- How digital cameras work (4 lectures)
- Photons, pixels, and bits (4 lectures)
- Interregnum (1 lecture)
- Color and Lighting (5 lectures)
- Image processing (2 lectures)

A set of references are also given as part of the lecture course [34]. These are included below and full acknowledgment is given to Prof Marc Levoy and Google Inc.

1. *London, B., Stone, J., Upton, J.: Photography, 11th edn. Pearson/Prentice Hall, New York (2011). 10th edition is better*
2. *Peterson, B.: Learning to See Creatively. Watson-Guptill, New York (1988) (or any later edition)*
3. *Hecht, E.: Optics, pp. 149–171, 4th edn. Pearson/Addison-Wesley, New York (2002). Chapter 5.1–5.2 – geometrical optics*
4. *Moller, T et al.: Real-Time Rendering, pp. 117–124, 3rd edn. AK Peters, Natick (2008). Chapter 5.6.1 – sampling and filtering theory*
5. *Goldberg, N.: The Dark Side of the Lens, pp. 35–50. Academic, Cambridge, MA (1992). Sections 1.11–1.20 – autofocus, etc*
6. *Adams, A.: Examples: The Making of 40 Photographs. Little Brown, New York (1983). Especially, pp. 40–43, 102–106, 107–111, 162–165*
7. *Stone, M.: A Field Guide to Digital Color, pp. 1–19. AK Peters, Natick (2003). Chapter 1, Color vision*
8. *Minneart, M.G.J.: Light and Color in the Outdoors, pp. 259–298. Springer, Berlin (1993). Chapter 11 (partial) – light and color of the sky*
9. *Reinhard, E., Ward, G., Pattanaik, S., Debevec, P.: High Dynamic Range Imaging; Acquisition, Display, and Image-Based Lighting, pp. 19–28. Elsevier, Amsterdam (2006). Chapter 2.1–2.2 – radiometry & photometry*
10. *Dorsey, J., Rushmeier, H., Sillion F.: Digital Modeling of Material Appearance, pp. 27–46. Elsevier, Amsterdam (2008). Chapter 3 – observation and classification*
11. *Hunter, F., Biver, S., Fuqua, P.: Light Science and Magic: An Introduction to Photographic Lighting, pp. 142–162, 4th edn. Focal Press, Waltham (1997). Chapter 7 (partial) – case study of glass [34]*

## 4.11   Ongoing Considerations with Regard to Digital Imaging

Photography remains a significant art form, and there are many exhibitions which display the work of famous photographers, including those who use modern digital technology as part of their work (e.g. David Hockney's use of the iPad).

However, today's smart phones have also made photographs more ubiquitous and transitory, and many have become an integral part of social media. Concerns have been expressed about the transitory nature of "point and shoot" images as they appear to be more to do with social communication and influence than the traditional values of photographic imaging, one of which has been to preserve significant images for posterity. However, some "point and shoot" images have become very important and influential because they were taken at the time of a significant national or international event that happened very quickly and no-one else was able to take any photographs. This is an example of how social media can determine the future in ways that may exceed the traditional methods of press reporting. It can preserve significant images for posterity.

It is clear that photography and imaging has to a certain extent been redefined from its origins – particularly in terms of its current contexts and social uses. The power and capability of modern digital cameras has also revealed detailed information in an image that the photographer was not aware of when the picture was taken.

Digital imaging has raised ongoing issues such as copyright, digital media rights, and fair use which are proving difficult to resolve. These are examined further in Chap. 8 on The Future.

A short list of books is included in Further Reading at the end of this chapter. The Bibliography at the end of this book includes a much longer list of Further Reading in the areas of –

• Image Manipulation
• Image Processing
• Image Compression
• Image Standards
• Special Effects
• Modeling
• Medical Imaging
• Robotics

## Further Reading

Ang, T.: Digital Photography Masterclass: Advanced Techniques for Creating Perfect Pictures 360, Dorling Kindersley, London (2017)
Bull, D.R.: Communicating Pictures: A Course in Image and Video Coding. 560, Academic, Oxford (2014)

DK: Digital Photography Complete Course. 360, Dorling Kindersley, Penguin Random House London (2015)

Harman, D.: The Digital Photography Handbook: An Illustrated Step by Step Guide, 224, Quercus, London. (2016)

Raskar, R., Tumblin, J.: Computational Photography: Mastering New Techniques for Lenses, Lighting, and Sensors. A.K. Peters, Natick (2010). https://en.wikipedia.org/wiki/History_of_ photography; https://en.wikipedia.org/wiki/Digital_camera

# References

1. Gavetti, G.M., Henderson, R., Giorgi, S.: Kodak and the Digital Revolution (A). Harvard Business School Case 705–448. (November 2004). (Revised November 2005). http://www.hbs.edu/faculty/Pages/item.aspx?num=31757

2. http://erickimphotography.com/blog/2013/10/29/street-photography-composition-lesson-6-framing/

3. https://en.wikipedia.org/wiki/Selfie

4. http://www.makeuseof.com/tag/5-camera-technologies-will-change-way-take-pictures/; http://www.techradar.com/news/photography-video-capture/cameras/best-camera-1271079; https://www.lifewire.com/cameras-of-the-future-493442

5. https://www.selva3d.com/; https://www.sculpteo.com/blog/2016/01/20/turning-a-picture-into-a-3d-model/; http://www.instructables.com/id/3D-Print-Your-Drawings/; https://www.shapeways.com/tutorials/how-to-use-2d-3d-app-convert-images-3d-models; http://make3d.cs.cornell.edu/; https://en.wikipedia.org/wiki/3D_reconstruction_from_multiple_images

6. Allen, P., Feiner, S., Troccoli, A., Benko, H., Ishak, E. Smith, B.: Seeing into the past: creating a 3D modeling pipeline for archaeological visualization. In: Proceedings of the 2nd International Symposium on 3D Data Processing, Visualization, and Transmission. IEEE Computer Society, New York (2004). http://ieeexplore.ieee.org/abstract/document/1335391/?reload=true; http://www.cs.columbia.edu/~allen/PAPERS/3dpvt04.1.pdf

7. https://en.wikipedia.org/wiki/Light-field_camera

8. https://illum.lytro.com/illum; http://graphics.stanford.edu/papers/lfcamera/; http://stanford.edu/class/ee367/reading/Ren%20Ng-thesis%20Lytro.pdf

9. http://videopreservation.conservation-us.org/BHoIT.pdf

10. https://en.wikipedia.org/wiki/Magnetic_resonance_imaging

11. https://newrepublic.com/article/119431/how-digital-cinema-took-over-35mm-film; https://en.wikipedia.org/wiki/History_of_film

12. https://en.wikipedia.org/wiki/Streaming_media

13. http://mentalfloss.com/article/49904/20-things-you-might-not-have-known-about-jurassic-park

14. http://www.hollywoodreporter.com/behind-screen/how-jurassic-park-revolutionized-visual-802332

15. http://www.businessinsider.com/how-cgi-works-in-jurassic-park-2014-7?IR=T

16. https://en.wikipedia.org/wiki/Special_effect

17. https://en.wikipedia.org/wiki/Computer_animation

18. https://en.wikipedia.org/wiki/Special_effect

19. https://www.wired.com/2015/05/inside-ilm/; http://www.ilm.com/; https://en.wikipedia.org/wiki/Industrial_Light_%26_Magic

20. http://www.pixar.com/; https://en.wikipedia.org/wiki/Pixar; https://en.wikipedia.org/wiki/List_of_Pixar_films

21. https://en.wikipedia.org/wiki/DreamWorks; http://dreamworkspictures.com/; https://www.forbes.com/companies/dreamworks-animation/

22. Earnshaw, R.A.: Art, Design and Technology: Collaboration and Implementation. Springer (2017)
23. https://www.gimp.org/
24. https://en.wikipedia.org/wiki/Blog
25. https://blogging.org/; https://www.blogger.com/about/?r=1-null_user
26. https://en.wikipedia.org/wiki/Video_blog; http://whatis.techtarget.com/definition/vlog-video-blog
27. http://www.huffingtonpost.co.uk/2014/12/17/25-vloggers-under-25-who-are-owning-the-world-of-youtube_n_6340280.html
28. Casey Neistat https://www.youtube.com/playlist?list=PLTHOlLMWEwVy52FUngq91krMk QDQBagYw
29. http://www.vlognation.com/how-to-start-a-vlog/; http://www.wikihow.com/Be-a-Vlogger
30. http://www.techradar.com/news/photography-video-capture/cameras/best-camera-1271079; www.techradar€.com/news/photography-video-capture/cameras/what-camera-should-i-buy-our-step-by-step-guide-helps-you-choose-1300667
31. http://www.techradar.com/news/photography-video-capture/cameras/best-compact-camera-2013-34-reviewed-963985
32. https://sites.google.com/site/marclevoylectures/home
33. https://www.youtube.com/user/marclevoy/videos;https://www.youtube.com/playlist?list=PL7 ddpXYvFXspUN0N-gObF1GXoCA-DA-7i
34. https://sites.google.com/site/marclevoylectures/schedule

# Chapter 5
# Digital Libraries

**Abstract** The digital revolution is having effects on the development, organization, and distribution of information and artefact repositories such as libraries, and the way in which physical and digital aspects are mediated to users. It was clear from the early involvement of the National Science Foundation (NSF), Defense Advanced Research projects Agency (DARPA) and National Aeronautics and Space Administration (NASA) in the USA that any developments in this area were going to be potentially significant for the future of large scale information retrieval of digital objects such as text, images, audio, and video. A review of library and related provision in higher education in the UK was commissioned in 1992 and reported on at the end of 1993. Many academic institutions and organizations have developed their own Institutional Repositories in order to store their own content. The advantages of digital libraries are summarized. The Google Digitization Project to digitize the world's information is reviewed and evaluated. Recent significant difficulties with the Project are summarized. There also current issues in ensuring digital archives remain accessible to users into the long term future and are not rendered obsolete by future shifts in technology. The changes that digital media and digital convergence are bringing about are substantial and are also likely to be long-lasting.

**Keywords** Digital computing • Large scale information retrieval • Digital objects • Institutional repositories • Google digitization project • Digital archives • Quality control • Copyright infringement • Bibliographic databases • Collective licensing • Long term digital preservation

## 5.1 Introduction

*The digital revolution is far more significant than the invention of writing or even of printing.*
Douglas Engelbart, 1997 [1]
*In 20 or 30 years, you'll be able to hold in your hand as much computing knowledge as exists now in the whole city, or even the whole world.* Douglas *Engelbart* [2]

© The Author(s) 2017                                                                                                 45
R. Earnshaw, *State of the Art in Digital Media and Applications*, SpringerBriefs in Computer Science, DOI 10.1007/978-3-319-61409-0_5

Various forms of calculating device were in operation at least from the time of Babbage in 1833, but it was not until the first stored program computers (ENIAC, 1946, and EDSAC, 1949, and the Manchester Mk1, 1949) that a more generalized form of operation was possible. The output of alphanumeric results of calculations on to printers was followed by output on to storage tubes and plotters in the 1960s. The use of computers was primarily for numerical calculations. However, there were early visions of a wider use of computers, though many of these visions were not universally shared until they had been successfully implemented. Thus there was widespread uncertainty in the early days about how computer technology and applications would develop and what forms these would take.

## 5.2  Digital Media Considerations

The Digital Media Alliance, Florida, defined digital media as *"the creative convergence of digital arts, science, technology and business for human expression, communication, social interaction and education"*.[3] Many traditional media companies now generate their content in digital form for distribution via CD, DVD, or the Internet, as well as print. Marketing strategies for content increasingly utilize multiple media channels to hit different markets simultaneously. New media forms such as wikis, blogs, podcasts, and the distribution of user-generated content (e.g. YouTube) are all changing the nature of information and how it is stored, updated, distributed, and accessed. Filtering, accreditation, and synthesis of content can be created through new hierarchies of peers and information affinity groups on the Internet.

## 5.3  Initial Developments in Digital Libraries

The term digital libraries first came to prominence by the Digital Libraries Initiative of NSF/DARPA/NASA in the USA 1994 [4]. It was clear from the early involvement of NSF, DARPA and NASA that any developments in this area were going to be potentially significant for the future of large scale information retrieval of digital objects (e.g. such as text, images, audio, and video).

In the UK, a review took place in 1992–93 by Sir Brian Follett [5]. It was the first general review of library provision in the UK since a report in 1967 by the Committee on Libraries established by the UK University Grants Committee in 1963.

A review of library and related provision in higher education in the UK was commissioned in 1992 and reported on at the end of 1993. It was chaired by Sir Brian Follett and the primary aim of the group that was set up was to review:

- *the implications of the growth in undergraduate student numbers for library services*

- *the role of libraries in support of research, given the increasing number of periodicals and specialist books, and their increase in price*
- *the developments in information technology and the implications for libraries.*

*It was the first general review of library provision since a report in 1967 by the Committee on Libraries established by the University Grants Committee in 1963 [5].*

  *The Follett Report [6] noted the shift that was starting from libraries as containers of information to information access. It was recognised that it was no longer possible for any single library to contain all the resources required. Shortfalls in space for libraries and materials were noted and urgent action was recommended, given the importance of libraries to the delivery of teaching and research. The Funding Councils accepted the Follett Report's findings and a sum of £10 million was made available in 1995 for building work in libraries related directly to student numbers. It was also recommended that the Funding Councils should jointly invest £20 million over three years in support of a series of development projects designed to further the use of IT in a number of areas. These included access and interfaces to national networks (e.g. the Joint Academic Network – JANET), navigational tools, electronic document storage and delivery, electronic journals, databases and datasets, library management systems, library automation, institutional information strategies, and training. The exploitation of IT was regarded as essential in creating the effective library of the future [5]*

A digital library is a repository where a significant proportion of the contents are in digital form. They are normally indexed and searchable via electronic means, which is an advantage over paper-based information. When the library is connected to the Internet, it can provide local and remote access with equal facility.

Many academic institutions and organizations have developed their own Institutional Repositories in order to store their own content that they have generated, such as PhD theses, academic research papers, and other works. These were generally open access (i.e. made freely available to the public via the Internet) in order to make the knowledge and information within the repository generally accessible and also to make as many people as possible aware of the value and quality of work being done in the institution. These may be viewed as digital libraries and are accessed in similar ways. Items can often be located by using a Google search on the Internet [7].

The advantages of the digital library include the following [7] –

- *No physical boundary*. *The user of a digital library need not to go to the library physically; people from all over the world can gain access to the same information, as long as an Internet connection is available.*
- *Round the clock availability* *A major advantage of digital libraries is that people can gain access 24/7 to the information.*
- *Multiple access*. *The same resources can be used simultaneously by a number of institutions and patrons. This may not be the case for copyrighted material: a library may have a license for "lending out" only one copy at a time; this is achieved with a system of digital rights management where a resource can become inaccessible after expiration of the lending period or after the lender chooses to make it inaccessible (equivalent to returning the resource).*

- *Information retrieval. The user is able to use any search term (word, phrase, title, name, subject) to search the entire collection. Digital libraries can provide very user-friendly interfaces, giving click able access to its resources.*
- *Preservation and conservation. Digitization is not a long-term preservation solution for physical collections, but does succeed in providing access copies for materials that would otherwise fall to degradation from repeated use. Digitized collections and born-digital objects pose many preservation and conservation concerns that analog materials do not. Please see the following "Problems" section of this page for examples.*
- *Space. Whereas traditional libraries are limited by storage space, digital libraries have the potential to store much more information, simply because digital information requires very little physical space to contain them and media storage technologies are more affordable than ever before.*
- *Added value. Certain characteristics of objects, primarily the quality of images, may be improved. Digitization can enhance legibility and remove visible flaws such as stains and discoloration.*
- *Easily accessible.* [7]

## 5.4   Large Scale Digital Libraries – The Google Digitization Project

Google's mission is *"to organize the world's information and make it universally accessible and useful"* [8]. It was therefore a logical development for Google to seek to digitize as much archive information as possible currently held in paper or book form in major world-leading universities and other leading organizations, and make it freely available globally over the Internet from its databases. The initial consortium in 2005 included Harvard, Stanford, University of Michigan, Oxford, New York Public Library, and Google. Google funded the work to be done, and at $10 per volume, the cost of digitization of 15 million books (the approximate size of the Harvard Library alone) was estimated at $150 million [9].

Although approximately 30 million books have been scanned by 2015 [10], there have been delays in the implementation of the project due to a number of factors including the following –

- Problems of quality control of the scanned text which has introduced many errors which have not been corrected.
- Legal challenges by authors and publishers on the grounds of alleged copyright infringements by Google.
- Fears that Google could create a monopoly in online, out-of-print books.
- Issue of trust with regard to Google's ultimate intentions for the project – was it to be non-profit and a service to the public, or did Google intend to utilize it in some way to generate revenue?

- Privacy issues to do with users accessing books anonymously, as they would do in a public library. This would not be possible to do if Google were intending to keep a record of books accessed in order to accrue data to feed into a business model of future plans.
- Google announced the intention in 2008 of including magazines and periodicals in its database and make them available to its book search. However, many traditional bibliographic databases make a clear distinction between books and periodicals.

One possible way forward was that proposed by the Authors Guild and involved extended collective licensing. It permitted the owners of scanned, out of print contents from libraries such as Google to make some of them available with payments to the authors [mm]. In November 2013, the presiding U.S. Circuit Judge dismissed *Authors Guild et al. v. Google.* On April 18, 2016, the Supreme Court turned down an appeal. *"It appears therefore that this decision was currently favoring Google, granting them the right to expand their digital library without violating the law"* [11].

## 5.5 Long Term Preservation of Digital Information

Digital information needs to remain readable and accessible into the long term future [12]. The Information Governance Initiative (IGI) produced a survey report in 2016, *"The Governance of Long-Term Digital Information: An IGI 2016 Benchmark"* [13]. The survey found that –

*while 98% of respondents had records that required long-term retention, only 11% of respondents were actually storing their records in a purpose-built long-term digital preservation system* [13].

In 1998 it was stated that digital preservation was essential for the future accessibility of information [14] –

*The critical role of digital ... archives in ensuring the future accessibility of information with enduring value has taken a back seat to enhancing access to current and actively used materials. As a consequence, digital preservation remains largely experimental and replete with the risks ... representing a time bomb that threatens the long-term viability of [digital archives]* [14].

In addition, around the same time the report of a task force on the archiving of digital information made a similar point [15]. The report called for a global effort to design and develop *"national information infrastructure to ensure that longevity of information is an explicit goal"* [15].

Little progress has been made in terms of a global infrastructure to provide a sustainable archive. In the meantime, there is increased national and international dependence on digital information, so the risk in this area has also increased as stated by the Information Governance Initiative [13] –

*Today, no such global infrastructure exists. And, although significant progress has been made to address the challenge by industry bodies, individual institutions, and providers of digital preservation technology, the existential and commercial threat represented by our accelerating and deepening reliance on digital information has only grown exponentially in the intervening 20 years* [13].

This is also reflected by statements in the press in 2015 [16] -

*We are nonchalantly throwing all of our data into what could become an information black hole without realizing it . . . documents or presentations that we've created may not be readable by the latest version of the software. So even if we accumulate vast archives of digital content, we may not actually know what it is* [16].

A report on the future of libraries has been produced by a task force at MIT in 2016 [17].

## 5.6   Conclusions

The development of digital libraries has been reviewed. Developments in the area in the area by NSF, DARPA and NASA in the USA in 1994 on the future of large scale information retrieval of digital objects (e.g. such as text, images, audio, and video) have been summarized. Similarly, the output of a review of library and related provision in higher education in the UK in 1993 by a committee chaired by Sir Brian Follett is summarized. It was the first general review of library provision in the UK since a report in 1967 by the Committee on Libraries established by the UK University Grants Committee in 1963. Many academic institutions and organizations have developed their own Institutional Repositories in order to store their own content. The advantages of digital libraries are summarized. The Google Digitization Project to digitize the world's information is reviewed and evaluated. Recent significant difficulties with the Project are summarized. There also current issues in ensuring digital archives remain accessible to users into the long term future and are not rendered obsolete by future changes in technology.

## Further Reading

Baker, D., Evans, W. (eds.): The End of Wisdom? The Future of Libraries in a Digital Age, pp. 238. Chandos Publishing, Cambridge (2016)

Deegan, M., Tanner, S. (eds.): Digital Preservation, pp. 288. Facet Publishing, London (2006)

Earnshaw, R.A., Vince, J.A.: Digital Convergence – Libraries of the Future, pp. 447. Springer, London (2008). ISBN: 13-978-1-84628-902-6. http://www.springer.com/gb/book/9781846289026

The Introduction is freely available online in the Front Matter. http://link.springer.com/book/10.1007%2F978-1-84628-903-3; http://link.springer.com/content/pdf/bfm%3A978-1-84628-903-3%2F1.pdf

Google Books. https://en.wikipedia.org/wiki/Google_Books

Google Books Library Project. https://www.google.com/googlebooks/library/

Google Book Search Settlement Agreement. https://en.wikipedia.org/wiki/Google_Book_Search_ Settlement_Agreement

Google Books Search Facility. https://books.google.com/

Google and the World Brain (video). https://www.youtube.com/watch?v=XZoLacp1-KE; https:// www.youtube.com/watch?v=4y43qwS8fl4

Lee, S.H.: Print vs Digital: The Future of Coexistence, pp. 158. Routledge, London (2016)

Logan R. K.: The Future of the Library: From Electric Media to Digital Media, pp. 238. Peter Lang Publishing Inc, Bern (2015)

Willinsky, J.: The Access Principle – The Case for Open Access to Research and Scholarship (2005). ISBN: 9780262232425 https://mitpress.mit.edu/books/access-principle; https://mit-press.mit.edu/books/series/digital-libraries-and-electronic-publishing

# References

1. Kitsantas, A., Dabbagh, N.: Learning to Learn with Integrative Learning Technologies (ILT): A Practical Guide for Academic Success, Chapter 20. Information Age Publishing, Charlotte (2013)
2. http://www.computinghistory.org.uk/pages/3972/In-20-or-30-years/;  http://www.azquotes.com/author/4505-Douglas_Engelbart
3. https://en.wikibooks.org/wiki/Intellectual_Property_and_the_Internet/Digital_media
4. Fox, E.A.: The digital libraries initiative – update and discussion. Bull. Am. Soc. Inf. Sci. **26**(1) (1999). http://www.asis.org/Bulletin/Oct-99/fox.html
5. Earnshaw, R.A., Vince, J.A.: Digital Convergence – Libraries of the Future, pp. 447, Springer, London (2008). ISBN: 13-978-1-84628-902-6. http://www.springer.com/gb/book/9781846289026. The above quotation is in the Introduction by the author and is freely available online in the Front Matter – http://link.springer.com/book/10.1007%2F978-1-84628-903-3; http://link.springer.com/content/pdf/bfm%3A978-1-84628-903-3%2F1.pdf
6. http://www.ukoln.ac.uk/services/papers/follett/report/
7. https://en.wikipedia.org/wiki/Digital_library
8. https://www.google.com/about/company/
9. https://dash.harvard.edu/bitstream/handle/1/4552061/suber_googlelibraryintro.htm?sequence=1; http://hul.harvard.edu/hgproject/;http://www.bodleian.ox.ac.uk/dbooks;https://www.liberquarterly.eu/articles/10.18352/lq.7853/; http://quod.lib.umich.edu/j/jahc/3310410.0007.305/--google-library?rgn=main;view=fulltext
10. http://www.newyorker.com/business/currency/what-ever-happened-to-google-books
11. https://en.wikipedia.org/wiki/Google_Book_Search_Settlement_Agreement;  https://en.wikipedia.org/wiki/Google_Books; https://phys.org/news/2016-04-supreme-court-google--online-library.html
12. http://www.lexology.com/library/detail.aspx?g=7170dd7d-43ce-4979-be91-cc9b3ccfd392
13. The Governance of Long Term Digital Information – IGI Benchmark 2016. http://preservica.com/wp-content/uploads/sites/3/2016/05/The-Governance-of-Long-Term-Digital-Information-IGI-Benchmark-2016.pdf
14. Hedstrom, M.: Digital preservation: a time bomb for digital libraries. Comput. Hum. **31**, 189–202 (1998) https://pdfs.semanticscholar.org/1f78/ff102bc627e675a8df7db2d996c69faad8cd.pdf
15. Preserving Digital Information: Report of the Task Force on Archiving of Digital Information. Commissioned by The Commission on Preservation and Access and The Research Libraries Group, pp. 71. https://www.clir.org/pubs/reports/pub63watersgarrett.pdf (May 1 1996)
16. Sample, I.: Google boss warns of 'forgotten century' with email and photos at risk. The Guardian, February 13, 2015. (Vincent Cerf, Internet pioneer; chief Internet evangelist at

Google) https://www.theguardian.com/technology/2015/feb/13/google-boss-warns-forgotten-century-email-photos-vint-cerf
17. Institute-wide Task Force on the Future of Libraries, pp. 28, MIT (2016). https://future-of-libraries.mit.edu/sites/default/files/FutureLibraries-PrelimReport-Final.pdf;   https://future-of-libraries.mit.edu/

# Chapter 6
# Applications of Digital Media

**Abstract** There are a wide range of digital media applications such as digital images, digital photography, digital video, digital audio, computer games, multimedia production, animation, digital video film making, e-books, web pages, data, and databases. Media content is now created in digital form and can be repurposed across different media types such as DVD, Internet, or traditional print. This offers scope for different forms of interactive media, and advertising, and providing added value to consumers by providing dynamic links to other relevant information. This provides new value chains and ecosystems. This is turn affects social and cultural contexts, and interacts with them. The user as content creator, publisher, and broadcaster is challenging and changing the traditional roles of news media, publishers, and entertainment corporations. This in turn changes social and governmental structures and affects their power, influence, and cultural impact. A number of Case Studies illustrate how the applications are developed and implemented in practice.

**Keywords** User as creator • Value chains • Repurposing media content • Digital heritage • Online book publishing • Interactive broadcasting • Vlogs • Disruptive technologies

## 6.1  Introduction

There is a wide range of application areas for digital media. This chapter can only give a snapshot and refer readers to the Further Reading and the References sections at the end of the chapter for more information.

Digital media applications areas include digital media applications such as digital images, digital photography, digital video, digital audio, digital libraries, computer games, multimedia production, animation, digital video film making, e-books, web pages, data, and databases. It could also include a range of applications where computing or multimedia is a component of an application such as embedded computing, the Internet of Things, smart clothing, 3D capture, motion capture, and digital heritage. Digital libraries are examined separately in Chap. 5 and social media in Chap. 7.

© The Author(s) 2017                                                                                    53
R. Earnshaw, *State of the Art in Digital Media and Applications*, SpringerBriefs in Computer Science, DOI 10.1007/978-3-319-61409-0_6

## 6.2   Digital Media Application Areas

Applications include the following domains –

- Creative industries
- Computational journalism
- Digital arts and culture
- Digital art
- Digital photography
- Media culture and digital content
- Film and video
- Video processing
- Virtual humans
- Digital storytelling
- Media and entertainment
- Virtual and augmented realities
- Interactions between media culture and digital content (e.g. [1])

  Digital tools include –

- Sentiment analysis
- Social media analytics – to provide quantitative data on how viewers are responding to media
  (e.g. the acquisition of Bluefin by Twitter for $90 million [2]

## 6.3   Applications Areas at MIT Media Laboratory

Initial research groups at the MIT Media Laboratory in 1987 included the following [3]–

- Electronic publishing
- Speech
- Advanced television research
- Moves of the future
- Visual languages
- Spatial imaging
- Computers and entertainment
- Animation and computer graphics
- Computer music
- School of the future
- Human-machine interface

Current research groups at the MIT Media Lab (2017) include the following [4] –

- *Affective computing – advanced wellbeing using new ways to communicate, understand, and respond to emotion*
- *Biomechatronics – enhancing human physical capability*
- *Camera culture – making the invisible visible – inside our bodies, around us, and beyond – for health, work, and connection*
- *Changing places – enabling dynamic, evolving places that respond to the complexities of life*
- *Civic media – creating technology for social change*
- *Conformable decoders – converting the patterns of nature and the human body into beneficial signals and energy*
- *Design fiction – sparking discussion about the social, cultural and ethical implications of emerging technologies through design and storytelling*
- *Fluid interfaces – integrating digital interfaces more naturally into our physical lives enabling insight, inspiration, and interpersonal connections*
- *Human dynamics – exploring how social networks can influence our lives in business, health, governance, and technology adoption and diffusion*
- *Lifelong kindergarten – engaging people in creative learning experiences*
- *Living mobile – enhancing mobile life through improved user interactions*
- *Macro connections – transforming data into knowledge*
- *Mediated matter – designing for, with, and by nature*
- *Molecular machines – engineering at the limits of complexity with molecular-scale parts*
- *Object-based media – changing storytelling, communication and everyday life through sensing, understanding, and new interface technologies*
- *Opera of the future – extending expression, learning and health through innovations in musical composition, performance, and participation*
- *Personal robots – building socially engaging robots and interactive technologies to help people live healthier lives, connect with others and learn better*
- *Playful systems – designing systems that become experiences to transcend utility and usability*
- *Responsive environments – augmenting and mediating human experience, interaction, and perception with sensor networks*
- *Scalable cooperation – reimagining the way society organizes, cooperates, and governs itself*
- *Sculpting evolution – exploring evolutionary and ecological engineering*
- *Signal kinetics – extending human and computer abilities in sensing, communication, and actuation through signals and networks*
- *Social computing – creating sociotechnical systems that shape our urban environments*
- *Social machines – understanding and empowering human networks*
- *Synthetic neurobiology – revealing insights into the human condition and repairing brain disorders via novel tools for mapping and fixing brain computations*

- *Tangible media – seamlessly coupling the worlds of bits and atoms by giving dynamic physical form to digital information and computation*
- *Viral communications – creating scalable technologies that evolve with user inventiveness* [4]

## 6.4  Case Studies

The following four Case Studies illustrate the diversity of applications that are possible with digital media. The first is a digital heritage project where historical sculptures were scanned to provide an archive that is available over the Internet. The second is an example of an independent online book publishing project where 750,000 copies of the novel were sold. The third is an interactive broadcasting pilot, where the viewers can provide feedback on the broadcast via computer. The final Case Study is in the area of videologs and short films. This company was acquired by CNN in November 2016.

### *6.4.1  Digital Michelangelo Project*

The Digital Michelangelo Project [5] by Stanford University performed a detailed high resolution scanning and analysis of statues and mosaics, and compiled an archive of 3D models which is made freely available over the Internet [6]. This project illustrated how technology could be utilized in an artistic application.

Laser scanning involves the control of a laser beam to measure distance, and capture the shape of a 3D object, such as a statue, building, or landscape. This process is controlled by software running on a computer and the scanned object is stored in digital form. This may then be analyzed or modified using CAD software, or more specialized applications. The project focused on producing a scan of David by Michelangelo (Fig. 6.1) using laser scanning.

A further scanning project was the digitization of the fragments of the Forma Urbis Romae [7]. This was a giant map of Rome that was carved on to marble slabs around 200 A.D. This map has been broken into 1163 pieces that have proved very difficult to piece together because of the large number of possible combinations. However, as the pieces are several inches thick, each surface on a fragment provides 3D information for optimally fitting the pieces together by appropriate computer algorithms.

It is also possible to generate a 3D model from photographs and images using specialized software [8].

**Fig. 6.1** David by Michelangelo Courtesy of Jörg Bittner Unna, David by Michelangelo (Detail), Florence, Galleria dell'Accademia, 1501–1504 https://en.wikipedia.org/wiki/David_ (Michelangelo)#/media/File:%27David%27_by_Michelangelo_Fir_JBU013.jpg By Jörg Bittner Unna (Own work) [CC BY 3.0 (http://creativecommons.org/licenses/by/3.0)], via Wikimedia Commons

### 6.4.2   Making a £Million from an Independently Published Digital Novel

Former barrister L. J. Ross rejected traditional offers and published independently online through Amazon [9]. On January 1, 2015, the novel "Holy Island" was published. By May 2015 it was in the No 1 position in Amazon's Kindle bestsellers list. 750,000 copies were sold at approx. £3–4. E-books have launched the careers of a number of authors including E.L. James, L. Genova, and A. Weir, whose novel "The Martian" was also made into a film. Of course, this is only one side of the story. We do not know what the sales and income would have been for publication using traditional publishers. Thus there is nothing to compare the above figures with, and whether they are significant by comparison or not. However, the current higher royalties available via Amazon Kindle (stated to be up to 70%) does offer a significantly higher return to the author than that from traditional publishers.

### 6.4.3   Virtual Interactive Studio Television Application Using Networked Graphical Supercomputers

Allowing users to interact with broadcast television programs offers an additional level of engagement and entertainment. The main objective of the VISTA project [10] was the integration and demonstration of a system to support the generation of scenarios for real-time interactive television. This realization of a virtual interactive studio offered facilities for mixing real and synthetic objects and characters in any combination, to be controlled remotely by end users such as home television viewers. The system enabled the realization of innovative interactive domestic teleservices. The image content of the programs was generated via Asynchronous Transfer Mode (ATM) in real-time by high-end graphical computers. To reduce costs, telephone networks were used for viewer feedback. The number of simultaneous interactive viewers varied from a few to several hundred. Three concrete and specific applications were tested using the system:

- An interactive television drama (simultaneously on three channels) with viewer participation
- Creation of a virtual presenter who can be controlled remotely in real-time.
- Creation of an interactive virtual driving environment to teach traffic rules.

Broadcasting companies were able to transmit interactive programs in which viewers could actively direct and participate. The project built on the expertise and technology of the HUMANOID, HUMANOID-2, CHARM, VISINET and VLNet projects. Further information is provided in [11].

Project Partners included – European Design Centre, BRTN, EPFL, Limburgs Universitair Centrum, NOB Interactive, University of Bradford, University of Geneva, VPRO Televisie, and Androme.

### *6.4.4   Video Logs and Short Films – Casey Neistat*

Case Neistat [12] was a daily video logger, short film maker, and co-founder of the social media company Berne, reported as being bought by CNN for $25 million in November 2016. Around the same time it was reported that the daily vlog was being replaced by short films to be published in his YouTube channel [13]. A number of the vlogs have become famous for the influence they have had on the behavior of companies with defective products (e.g. Apple and its batteries for the iPod) with the video "iPod's Dirty Secret", the difficulties with the New York Police Department's ticketing of cyclists in New York City for not using bike lanes (in the video "Bike Lanes"), or to advertise a particular company in a new way (e.g. Nike) with the video "Make it Count". The effect that short videos such as these have had on millions of viewers has been substantial and demonstrates the power of video with effective story boarding and production techniques. Neistat has participated in a number of detailed interviews where he sets out his personal approach to his work. These are included in Table 6.1.

## 6.5   Disruptive Effect of Digital Technology on Traditional Businesses

Digital technology has had a disruptive effect on traditional business from the very first computer. Those companies and organizations that could adapt quickly were able to achieve the greatest benefits.

A number of factors can affect businesses in this situation. If there is a low barrier to entry into the sector of a particular business, then this could allow a more agile competitor who is able to take advantage of the new technology to quickly move in and develop market share at the expense of more traditional companies. The second factor is the legacy business models of the more traditional companies which have been developed since the company was first formed. These could contain embedded organizational and cultural challenges which may be very difficult to change at the speed that is required to exploit the new technology [14, 15].

An example in the area of digital media is how streaming media suddenly provided services to the customer that enabled them to access digital content directly over the Internet rather than have to go through a cable company. The rapid growth of streaming video (e.g. Netflix) has demonstrated how effective an attractive new service can be. It inevitably places existing providers under pressure.

A variety of sources provide a number of principles of best practice to enable companies to address the challenges caused by rapid developments in the field of digital technology. These include the following considerations –

- Consider bringing in a Chief Technology Officer at board level to catalyze the changes needed

**Table 6.1**  A Selection of videos created by Casey Neistat

| Video Title | Duration | Objective and content | No of viewers | Recognition |
|---|---|---|---|---|
| iPod's Dirty Secret – Casey Neistat – ORIGINAL VIDEO (2003) – YouTube | 2 min 57 s | Apple's lack of battery replacement for the iPod | 1.2 million | The publicity generated by the video caused Apple to change its policy |
| Bike Lanes by Casey Neistat – YouTube | 3 min 3 s | Exposed the problems with bike lanes in New York city and associated fines by the police | 18 million | Substantial publicity for blocked bike lanes and the problems they cause |
| Make It Count – YouTube | 4 min 37 s | Unusual approach to a publicity video for Nike | 25 million | Generated a lot of interest in the Nike brand |
| Casey Neistat on Writing Your Own Rules – with Lewis Howes | 1 h 9 min 49 s | Explains his work strategy | 259,000 | |
| THE BEST CAMERA MONEY CAN BUY | 7 min 2 s | Casey Neistat explains his requirements for a good camera for his work | 2.3 million | Publicity for his chosen camera and how it is used in practice |
| Casey Neistat – VidCon talk 2016 | 24 min 45 s | Update | 420,000 | |
| THE $21,000 FIRST CLASS AIRPLANE SEAT – YouTube | 9 min 5 s | Publicity video | 32 million | |
| Casey Neistat's Top 10 Rules For Success (@ CaseyNeistat) | 6 min 1 s | Top 10 rules to follow | 89,000 | |
| Casey Neistat Interview (Full Episode) | The Tim Ferriss Show (Podcast) Tim Ferriss | 1 h 39 min 51 s | Interview | 33,000 | |
| Casey Neistat's Wildly Functional Studio | 16 min 37 s | Casey Neistat's office/work space | 2.6 million | Modern studio for the production process |
| Sundance – How & Why to Use YouTube Casey Neistat | 57 min 51 s | How and Why to use YouTube | 32,000 | |
| Total 490 videos | | | Total 170 million | |

URLs for the above videos in the table are as follows –
iPod's Dirty Secret https://www.youtube.com/watch?v=RKT7RzYBN5I
Bike Lanes https://www.youtube.com/watch?v=bzE-IMaegzQ

(continued)

**Table 6.1** (continued)

Make it Count https://www.youtube.com/watch?v=WxfZkMm3wcg
Writing your own Rules – with Lewis Howes https://www.youtube.com/watch?v=NAp-BIXzpGA
The Best Camera Money can Buy https://www.youtube.com/watch?v=FvhOwpip0K8
VidCon talk 2016 https://www.youtube.com/watch?v=KlJnsHpWamU
The $21,000 First Class Airplane Seat https://www.youtube.com/watch?v=84WIaK3bl_s
Top 10 Rules for Success https://www.youtube.com/watch?v=NjuUXYZf4DY
Interview on the Tim Ferriss show https://www.youtube.com/watch?v=vB0Mz8iHDyU
Casey Neistat's wildly Functional Studio https://www.youtube.com/watch?v=vb60rrtTddQ
How and Why to use YouTube https://www.youtube.com/watch?v=qnLMKxuBeCw

- Consider carefully the portfolio of skills needed to accomplish change, in the areas of the company where this is required
- Ensure the company considers the data it needs to support and develop its business
- Ensure the company is focused on what its customers want, and what data is needed to ensure this happens
- If the traditional business loses market share to more agile competitors who are more successful in utilizing new technology, consider what alternative revenue streams might be generated [15]

## 6.6   Conclusions

Digital media applications have been summarized. A number of Case Studies have been described which illustrate the diversity and wide range of application domains. Further information on these Case Studies and other application domains are provided in the References and Further Reading.

## Further Reading

Cunningham, S., Berry D., Earnshaw, R.A., Excell, P.S., Thompson, E.: Multi-disciplinary creativity and collaboration: utilizing crowd-accelerated innovation and the internet. In: Proceedings of International Conference on Cyberworlds, IEEE Computer Society, Washington, DC (2015). http://ieeexplore.ieee.org/document/7398427/. doi:10.1109/CW.2015.29
Earnshaw, R.A., Vince, J.A. (eds.): Intelligent Agents for Mobile and Virtual Media, pp. 195. Springer, London (2002) ISBN: 1-85233-5564. For more information see: http://www.amazon.co.uk/Intelligent-Agents-Mobile-Virtual-ebook/dp/B001BPEWJI
Earnshaw, R.A., Vince, J.A. (eds.): Digital Content Creation, pp. 354. Springer, London. ISBN: 1-85233-379-0 (2001). http://www.springer.com/computer/image+processing/book/978-1-85233-379-9 http://www.springer.com/gb/book/9781852333799

Earnshaw, R.A., Magnenat-Thalmann, N., Terzopoulos, D., Thalmann, D.: Computer animation for virtual humans, IEEE Comput. Graph. Appl. IEEE Comput. Soc. 18(5), 20–23. (1998). http://ieeexplore.ieee.org/document/708557/. doi:10.1109/MCG.1998.708557

Earnshaw, R.A.: 3D and multimedia on the information superhighway. IEEE Comput. Graph. Appl. IEEE Comput. Soc. 17(2), 30–31 (1997). http://ieeexplore.ieee.org/document/574673/. doi:10.1109/MCG.1997.574673

Earnshaw, R.A., Jones, H., Vince, J.A. (eds.): Virtual Reality Applications pp. 328. Academic, London. ISBN: 0-12-227755-4 (1995). http://dl.acm.org/citation.cfm?id=214650

Joslin, C., Molet, T., Magnenat-Thalmann, N., Esmerado, J., Thalmann, D.: Sharing attractions on the net with VPARK. IEEE Comput. Graph. Appl. IEEE Comput. Soc. 21(1), 61–71 (2001). http://ieeexplore.ieee.org/document/895134/. doi:10.1109/38.895134

# References

1. Earnshaw, R.A., Robison D., Palmer I.J., Excell P.S.: Transformative interactions between media culture and digital content. In: Proceedings of International Conference on Internet Technologies and Applications, pp. 57–65 (2013). ISBN 978-0-946881-81-9
2. http://allthingsd.com/20130212/why-twitter-dropped-close-to-90-million-on-bluefin-labs/
3. Brand, S.: The Media Lab: Inventing the Future at MIT, p. 285. Viking Penguin Inc, New York (1987)
4. https://www.media.mit.edu/research/?filter=groups
5. Levoy, M., Pulli, K., Curless, B., Rusinkiewicz, S., Koller, D., Pereira, L., Ginzton, M., Anderson, S., Davis, J., Ginsberg, J., Shade, J., Fulk, D.: The digital michelangelo project: 3D scanning of large statues. In: Proceedings of the 27th Annual Conference on Computer Graphics and Interactive Techniques, pp. 131–144. ACM Press/Addison-Wesley Publishing Co, New York (2000). doi:10.1145/344779.344849. https://graphics.stanford.edu/papers/dmich-sig00/dmich-sig00-nogamma-comp-low.pdf. https://graphics.stanford.edu/papers/dmich-sig00/
6. https://graphics.stanford.edu/projects/mich/. http://graphics.stanford.edu/data/mich/. http://www.cs.cmu.edu/~seitz/course/SIGG99/papers/levoy-abs.pdf. http://illumin.usc.edu/printer/46/michelangelo39s-motion-picture/By/
7. https://graphics.stanford.edu/projects/mich/forma-urbis/forma-urbis.html
8. https://www.sculpteo.com/blog/2016/01/20/turning-a-picture-into-a-3d-model/. https://www.quora.com/What-software-is-best-for-generating-an-accurate-3D-model-from-2D-photos. https://en.wikipedia.org/wiki/3D_reconstruction_from_multiple_images
9. The Times, February 10, Section 2 Arts, pp. 4–5 (2017). http://www.thetimes.co.uk/article/the-barrister-who-writes-bestselling-digital-thrillers-75fsp7lfc. https://www.ljrossauthor.com/. https://lovesuspense.com/2017/02/
10. EU Esprit High Performance Computing – Project VISTA – Virtual Interactive Studio Television Application using Networked Graphical Supercomputers (EP22517). https://cordis.europa.eu/esprit/src/itfmrprj.htm#EP22517
11. Flerackers, C., Earnshaw, R.A., Vanischem, G., Van Reeth, F., Alsema, F.: Creating Broadcast Interactive Drama in a Networked Virtual Environment. IEEE Comput. Graph. Appl. IEEE Comput. Soc. 21(1), 56–60 (2001). http://ieeexplore.ieee.org/document/895133/. doi:10.1109/38.895133
12. https://en.wikipedia.org/wiki/Casey_Neistat
13. https://www.youtube.com/user/caseyneistat
14. https://www.edx.org/

15. https://hbr.org/2016/03/the-industries-that-are-being-disrupted-the-most-by-digital.     http://
    venturebeat.com/2014/05/15/digital-disruption-is-forcing-businesses-to-change-how-
    business-is-done/.     https://www.budde.com.au/Research/BuddeComm-Intelligence-Report-
    The-Media-Industry-and-the-Disruptive-Impact-of-Digital-Services.         http://www.up.ac.
    za/media/shared/404/ZP_Files/Innovate%2009/Articles/the-effect-of-digital-publishing.
    zp40045.pdf.         http://www.computerworld.com/article/2976572/emerging-technology/
    digital-disruption-from-the-perspective-of-porters-five-forces-framework.html.     http://www.
    mckinsey.com/industries/high-tech/our-insights/the-impact-of-disruptive-technology-a-
    conversation-with-eric-schmidt.         http://www.opentext.com/file_source/OpenText/en_US/
    PDF/Digital%20Disruption%20and%20the%20Digital%20Media%20Supply%20
    Chain%20WP.pdf

# Chapter 7
# Social Media and Cultural Implications

**Abstract** The use of digital media systems followed by progressive reliance on social media, appears to follow the law of sharing, an equivalent of Moore's law in the context of social media, where the average amount of information shared doubles every year. This baseline helps businesses to develop, and accelerate, commercial and social applications, and define business information handling requirements. Business use of Web 2.0 technologies, often referred to as Enterprise 2.0, may be defined as an organization's use of emergent social software platforms to pursue its goals. Enterprise 2.0 technologies offer business and governmental organizations the opportunity to improve their communications, processes, and ultimately performance. Creative industries are generally a collaborative activity involving many pathways and pipelines of delivery of their constituent parts. Therefore they depend on networking and connectivity between creators and distributors. The creative industries and digital media are also dominated by Small and Medium Enterprises (SMEs) and are heavily dependent on the networking of people and ideas. This combination also potentially provides additional value beyond traditional e-commerce activities due to the ability to form virtual customer environments. Other benefits include improved marketing and stronger customer relationships, and providing people and organizations with a platform to further pursue company objectives. However, the value in the use of social networking is not determined by the platforms themselves, but in how they are harnessed to create value for the organizations and participants. The risks and obstacles to organizational adoption and use of social networking and social media technologies need to be recognized. Principal concerns include sensitive or critical data appearing on a public-facing social network, data ownership, data protection, regulatory issues involving the cloud, and intellectual property. For Small and Medium Sized Enterprises (SMEs) the main challenges are in terms of the appropriate deployment of social media tools, and ensuring employees receive training in the responsible use of social media.

**Keywords** Creative industries • Creative clusters • Creative citizens • Cultural industries • Information society • Collaborative working • Arts and media policy • Social network markets • Virtual communities

© The Author(s) 2017
R. Earnshaw, *State of the Art in Digital Media and Applications*, SpringerBriefs in Computer Science, DOI 10.1007/978-3-319-61409-0_7

## 7.1  Introduction and Background

Increasingly, Web 2.0 social media tools in the form of consumer applications such as Facebook and Twitter are being used by billions of people for data sharing and free form crowd-driven patterns of activity. Social media enables users to create and share content or to participate in social networking by means of text, images, multimedia, websites and applications. In particular, they utilize computer-mediated technologies that allow individuals, groups of individuals, companies, governments, and other organizations to view, create and share information and ideas, and other forms of content. They are a form of virtual community exchanging information in virtual space. There are a number of social media services currently available aimed at different constituencies of potential users. However, there are a number of common features to many of them, including the following [1] –

1. interactive Web 2.0 Internet-based applications
2. user-generated content such as text posts or comments, multimedia, and data generated through online interactions
3. users create service-specific profiles for the website or app, which may be designed and maintained by the social media organization
4. development of online social networks by connecting a user's profile with those of other individuals and/or groups

## 7.2  Social Media

Social media is generally regarded as constituting an advance on traditional media in the areas of reach, frequency, usability, immediacy, and permanence. Social media provides a focus for social and professional communities of interest to share ideas and exchange information. Knowledge and information are therefore key drivers. However, there may be no editorial control over content or dissemination. Therefore the accuracy and provenance of the information is not guaranteed unless the recipient knows that the information is coming from a proven and reliable source.

Kaplan and Haenlein [2] defined social media as –

*A group of Internet-based applications that build on the ideological and technological foundations of Web 2.0 and that allow the **creation and exchange of user-generated content** (p. 61) [2].*

The degree of presence and user-experience afforded by the interaction and exchange of data is governed to a large extent by the type of information (e.g. text or multimedia) and the devices used (e.g. mobile phone or virtual reality headset). Text such as messages or blogs only allow for simple exchanges. Content communities may be regarded as being at a higher level (e.g. YouTube, Facebook) and share richer content such as images and videos. The current highest level is that provided by online gaming and 3D worlds which seek to reproduce in a virtual environment the characteristics of real-world experiences such as person-to-person interactions.

Carr and Hayes [3] defined social media as follows –

> Social media are **Internet-based** *channels that allow users to* **opportunistically interact** *and selectively* **self-present**, *either in* **real-time or asynchronously**, *with both* **broad and narrow audiences** *who derive value from* **user-generated content** *and the* **perception of interaction with others** (p. 50) [3].

Facebook was one of the first online social media and social networking services and was launched in 2004. It is one of the fastest growing companies and has 1.8 billion monthly active users in 2016.

Social media sites that can be used to maximize online presence include the following –

- Facebook
- Twitter
- Instagram
- YouTube
- Flickr
- Tumblr
- 500px
- DeviantArt
- WhatsApp
- Baidu Tieba
- Pinterest
- LinkedIn
- Google+
- Viber
- Snapchat
- Weibo
- WeChat
- Beme

The above websites have a total of more than eight billion registered users [4].

A 2007 research study conducted by researchers from Rice University, the University of Maryland, and Max Planck Institute for Software Systems analyzed the characteristics of very large online social networks in order to determine the origins and characteristics of their success. The research included Orkut, YouTube, MySpace, LinkedIn, and LiveJournal. The study observed that web pages are based on content whereas online social networks are based on users. A conclusion of the study was that the most trustworthy nodes, or members, of the network are those users who established the largest number of friends within the online network, establishing themselves as close to the core of that social network as possible. This implies that the degree of proximity to the core of a social network determines the speed of propagation of information to wider segments of the network. Clearly this has marketing implications for companies wishing to utilize social networks to offer products or services.

The characteristics of social networks are outlined in [5].

## 7.3   Creative Industries

Creative industries are generally a collaborative activity involving many pathways and pipelines of delivery of their constituent parts. Therefore they depends on networking and connectivity between creators and distributors. The creative industries and digital media are also dominated by Small and Medium Enterprises (SMEs) and are heavily dependent on the networking of people and ideas, as they may not have a particular expertise in house due to the limited size of the company.

Social media also provides a networked environment. It is also both local and global. It brings together people with common aims, objectives and interests – both social and commercial. Social media platforms can also provide the basis for the sharing and distribution of various types of digital media.

Creative industries and social media share the following characteristics –

* Interdependence
* Interactive
* Aggregation
* Publicity
* Communication
* Distribution
* Combining of assets
* User-centered
* Relationship-sustaining

The evolution of the creative industries has included creative clusters, creative citizens and social network markets.

Garnham [6] summarizes the creative industries as follows –

> *Creative industries have been understood in the context of information society … and draws its political and ideological power from the prestige and economic importance attached to concepts of innovation, information, information workers and the impact of information and communication technologies drawn from information society theory* [6]

Hartley [7] identifies the significance and importance of the creative industries as follows –

> *So the creative industries are important because they are clustered at the point of attraction for a billion or more young people around the world. They're among the drivers of demographic, economic and political change. They start from the individual talent of the creative artist and the individual desire and aspiration of the audience. These are the raw materials for innovation, change and emergent culture, scaled up to form new industries and coordinated into global markets based on social networks* [7].

Potts et al. [8] have proposed a new market-based definition of creative industries in terms of the extent to which supply and demand operate in complex social networks. This differs from the traditional definition based on the creative nature of inputs and the intellectual property contained in the outputs. They also discuss the empirical, analytic and policy implications of this new definition.

Social media has become central to businesses and its marketing of products and services to meet customer needs, whether directly or indirectly. A study by Optimum Research [9] found that 57% of small businesses utilized social media to support marketing [10]. Nineteen percent of businesses used Facebook and 14% LinkedIn. The primary objectives were to increase brand awareness (27%) and to boost sales (15%).

The creative class has been identified by Richard Florida as a driving force in economic development [11]. In turn, this includes a highly creative core including media workers. Those who include technology to drive and implement this creativity in transformational ways may be regarded as the new creatives.

## 7.4   Traditional Media and Social Media

Table 7.1 summarizes the differences between traditional media and digital/social media. Optimizing the balance between the two in terms of meeting the needs of readers and users is the challenge for current approaches. In addition, the advertisers and other generators of revenue examine the returns from their utilization of the two approaches, and make decisions about future allocations based on current trends. Further, social media allows the distribution of news without it being filtered by the traditional approaches that news media and editors may adopt [12].

**Table 7.1**   Traditional media versus digital/social media production

| Process | Traditional media | Digital/social media |
| --- | --- | --- |
| Production | Official Channels only | Read & Write web → DIY |
| | Professional/specialized | |
| | Gatekeepers | |
| Creation | Standardized | Creative/eclectic |
| | Conservative | Disruptive |
| | Concentration of power | Distribution of power |
| Distribution | One way communication | Multi-way communication |
| | Impersonal | Personalized |
| | | Networked |
| | | Community focused |
| | | Interactive |

Courtesy of Christina Costa
http://www.slideshare.net/cristinacost/creative-industries-social-media
License: CC Attribution-NonCommercial-ShareAlike License

**Table 7.2**  Facebook, YouTube, Twitter, and Instagram at 2015

|         | Facebook | YouTube | Twitter | Instagram |
|---------|----------|---------|---------|-----------|
| Users | 1.44 billion monthly active users | 1 billion | 302 million monthly active users | 400 million monthly active users |
|       | 1.25 billion mobile active users | | | |

Statistics courtesy of [13]

**Table 7.3**  Facebook, YouTube, Twitter, and Instagram at 2016

|         | Facebook | YouTube | Twitter | Instagram |
|---------|----------|---------|---------|-----------|
| Users | 1.79 billion monthly active users | 1.3 billion | 317 million monthly active users | 500 million monthly active users |
|       | 1.57 billion mobile active users | | | |
| Activity | | 3.25 billion hours watched per month | 500 million tweets per day | |
|          | | 10,000 YouTube videos generated 1 billion views | | |
| % Increase from 2015 to 2016 | 24% | 30% | 5% | 25% |

Statistics courtesy of [14]

## 7.5   Utilization of Facebook, Twitter, YouTube, and Instagram

Tables 7.2 and 7.3 show the number of users of Facebook, YouTube, Twitter, and Instagram in 2015 and 2016. Thus use of the Internet and associated social media shows continued growth.

Data associated with the use of social media can be used to identify clients, users, market trends, and future market opportunities [15].

## 7.6   Challenges of Social Media Environments

There are a number of potential risks and obstacles to organizational adoption and use of social networking and social media technologies. These include the possibility of company sensitive data appearing on a public-facing social network, data ownership, data protection, regulatory issues involving the cloud, and intellectual property rights.

For Small and Medium Sized Enterprises (SMEs) the main challenges are in terms of the appropriate deployment of social media tools, and ensuring employees receive training in the responsible use of social media.

## 7.7  Lessons Learned

A report on the new creatives by Adobe Inc. in 2014 [16] identified a number of ways in which those involved in developing creative applications have responded to the challenges and opportunities of the rapidly changing and expanding digital environment. This included the following [16] –

- *80% believe they must learn new tools and techniques and three quarters say that creatives must now work across multiple mediums and disciplines*
- *An overwhelming majority (77%) of creatives believe change within the industry is happening rapidly, with two-thirds expecting their role to be significantly different within 3 years*
- *74% of creatives view mobile technology as transforming the face of creativity and design and 7 in 10 creatives are developing content for mobile apps*
- *87% believe creating mobile content has had a positive impact on them*
- *While creatives still rely on pen and paper for ideation (28%) and brainstorming (36%), nearly half (45%) use their mobile devices to capture inspiration on-the-go*
- *42% say they use mobile to create content anywhere*
- *30% of respondents would like to create more content on tablets, surpassing desktop computers*
- *App development (20%) and 3D modeling (18%) will be the most in-demand skills over the next 12 months*
- *Over twice as many creatives see digital sources, such as social media (36%), as the best sources of inspiration, compared to more traditional sources like fashion or architecture*
- *Creatives are also turning to professional online communities, noting inspiration (27%), collaboration and sharing (26%) as top reasons for participating*
- *While still mostly trusting their gut (79%) to make creative decisions, creatives view the impact of technology and digital analytics positively: 75% note that technology gives them more control over their professional destiny and 70% feel empowered by analytics [16]*

## 7.8  Conclusions

Social media is having a significant and transformative effect on communications and there are substantial implications for businesses, economics, and politics. It demonstrates continued growth and expansion, and its long term impact is therefore likely to be substantial. Businesses such as creative industries rely heavily on networks and can benefit substantially from an optimum use of social media. Data associated with a network can assist in expanding business opportunities. In addition, new techniques in visual and semantic analytics are being developed in order to accomplish more detailed analyses. Key issues are scale, complexity, and speed, and the challenge of handling unstructured data.

## Further Reading

Adobe: The New Creatives Report, p. 28 (2014) http://www.adobe.com/content/dam/Adobe/en/solutions/digital-media/pdfs/adobe-new-creatives-report.pdf

Acker, O., Grone, F., Lefort, T., Kropiunigg, L.: The Digital Future of Creative Europe: the Impact of Digitization and the Internet on the Creative Industries in Europe, p. 84 (2015) http://www.strategyand.pwc.com/media/file/The-digital-future-of-creative-Europe-2015.pdf

Howkins, J.: The Creative Economy: How People Make Money from Ideas, p. 304. Penguin, London (2013)

Martin, A., van Bavel, R.: Assessing the Benefits of Social Networks for Organizations. JRC Technical Reports, p. 34. European Commission (2013) http://ftp.jrc.es/EURdoc/JRC78641.pdf

Timeline of social media. https://en.wikipedia.org/wiki/Timeline_of_social_media

## References

1. Obar, J.A., Wildman, S.: Social media definition and the governance challenge: An introduction to the special issue. Telecommun. Policy. **39**(9), 745–750 (2015). doi:10.1016/j.telpol.2015.07.014

2. Kaplan, A.M., Haelein, M.: Users of the world, unite! The challenges and opportunities of Social Media. Business Horizons, vol. 53, pp. 59–68. Elsevier (2010). https://www.scribd.com/doc/63799736/Kaplan-and-Haenlein-2010-Social-Media

3. Carr, C.T., Hayes, R.A.: Social Media: Defining, Developing, and Divining. Atl. J. Commun. **23**(1), 46–65 (2015). doi:10.1080/15456870.2015.972282

4. https://www.statista.com/statistics/272014/global-social-networks-ranked-by-number-of-users/

5. http://socialnetworking.lovetoknow.com/Characteristics_of_Social_Networks

6. Garnham, N.: From Cultural to Creative Industries: An analysis of the implications of the 'creative industries' approach to arts and media policy making in the United Kingdom. Int. J. Cult. Policy. **11**(1), 15–29 (2005)

7. Hartley, J.: The evolution of the creative industries – creative clusters, creative citizens and social network markets. In: Proceedings of the Creative Industries Conference. Asia-Pacific Weeks, Berlin (2007). https://core.ac.uk/download/pdf/10882075.pdf?repositoryId=310

8. Potts, J., Cunningham, S., Hartley, J., Ormerod, P.: Social network markets: a new definition of the creative industries. J. Cult. Econ. **32**(3), 167–185 (2008). doi:10.1007/s10824-008-9066-y. http://link.springer.com/article/10.1007/s10824-008-9066-y
9. http://www.hiscox.co.uk/business-insurance/tips-and-information/how-businesses-use-socialmedia/
10. http://www.theguardian.com/media-network/2014/dec/02/tips-marketers-social-media-increase-engagement
11. https://en.wikipedia.org/wiki/Creative_classhttps://en.wikipedia.org/wiki/Creative_class
12. https://multimedia.journalism.berkeley.edu/tutorials/digital-transform/
13. http://venturebeat.com/2015/04/22/facebook-passes-1-44b-monthly-active-users-1-25b-mobile-users-and-936-million-daily-users/;http://tubularinsights.com/youtube-facts-stats-2014/; https://www.statista.com/statistics/282087/number-of-monthly-active-twitter-users/
14. https://www.statista.com/statistics/264810/number-of-monthly-active-facebook-users-world-wide/; https://www.statista.com/statistics/282087/number-of-monthly-active-twitter-users/; http://fortunelords.com/youtube-statistics/; https://www.statista.com/statistics/253577/number-of-monthly-active-instagram-users/
15. https://fstoppers.com/business/how-social-media-changing-creative-industry-91072
16. Adobe Inc.: The New Creatives Report, p. 28 (2014). http://www.adobe.com/content/dam/Adobe/en/solutions/digital-media/pdfs/adobe-new-creatives-report.pdf

# Chapter 8
# The Future

**Abstract** The domain of digital media and its applications is a complex mix of technical, social, cultural and legal aspects, so it is difficult to predict the future. However, looking at current trends in traditional businesses and the formation of new businesses that have a significant effect on the market place, can act as a guide on how digital media is likely to develop in the future. It is a given that in the foreseeable future technology is going get cheaper, smaller, and more powerful. However, the chip manufacturers are currently predicting that in 5–10 years' time the limits to silicon technology may result in a switch to alternative technologies.

There are differences of view in the community and industry on aspects of digital media in a number of areas including copying, fair use, and digital rights management. Some of these have become ongoing legal issues and associated court cases and have proved very difficult to resolve. This suggests that the statutory laws for traditional physically based media do not transition easily to digital-based media and may need to be revised and updated for the new digital environments.

There are current issues with the long-term preservation of digital archives and devising methods to ensure that future changes in technology do not result in current technologies and their associated information and databases becoming obsolete.

**Keywords** Copying and redistribution of digital media • Digital adverts • Push and pull content • Long-term preservation • Digital rights management

## 8.1 Introduction

*"The best way to predict the future is to invent it"* Alan Kay [1]

Predicting the future is difficult if not impossible. In addition, the domain of digital media and its applications is a complex mix of technical, social, cultural and legal aspects.

The main problem with silicon circuity on the chip appears to be the physical limits to further shrinking and the heat generated by the circuitry which cannot easily be dispersed from such small spaces [2].

© The Author(s) 2017
R. Earnshaw, *State of the Art in Digital Media and Applications*, SpringerBriefs in Computer Science, DOI 10.1007/978-3-319-61409-0_8

## 8.2   Trends in Digital Media

Consumption of content via traditional TV appears to be declining with time, particularly among younger viewers [3], which in turn has reduced the amount companies spend on advertising. Younger viewers watch content on smart phone, iPad, and laptop, i.e. mobile devices.

Consumers of TV content also seem to be moving away from traditional TV content to on-demand services such as Netflix, Hulu, Amazon Prime, and YouTube, resulting in the traditional content providers, such as Comcast, Dish, and Time Warner, losing customers [4].

It appears that consumers are moving in the direction of pull content rather than tuning into push content which is completely under the control of the broadcaster. Viewers now wish to be more in control of what they want to view, and when and how they wish to view it.

eMarketer, the leading research firm for marketing in a digital world, did an analysis of the current situation in its Global Media Intelligence Report 2016 (31 Jan 2017) [5] –

*For example, in the United States:*

- *Television is the most widespread content-based medium in the nation, as 89.1% of adults watched at least one half hour of free-to-air or cable television during a typical week in Spring 2016.*
- *Internet penetration reached 81.7% of the adult population in Spring 2016.*
- *Nearly 80% of adults had listened to radio, but just 18.1% had done so through the Internet or apps.*
- *72.4% of respondents had read a print magazine during an average month in Spring 2016.*
- *46.3% of adults had read a print newspaper in the last month, and 21.3% had read a daily newspaper.*
- *Social media usage was more common among females than males at 71.7% to 60.2%.*
- *Nearly 56% of males had watched a YouTube video in the last 30 days, compared to 49.6% of females.*
- *More than 95% of adults had a mobile phone in Spring 2016, and 77.6% had a smartphone. And 45.1% had a tablet or e-reader.*
- *71.6% of adults had gone online with a mobile phone or smartphone in the last month, which surpassed the 69.8% who had done so with a laptop or desktop [5]*

On 7 December 2016, the CEO of Business Insider summarized the future of digital media as follows [6] –

- *Digital is taking over. Every other media is shrinking. Mobile is growing.*
- *Generational shift – younger (18–24 years) not watching linear TV – down 40% in last 5 years*
- *Digital adverts are growing.*

- *Google, Facebook dominate the market place– followed everybody else. Need another big players*
- *20% growth in advertising revenues. Google revenues up 23%, Facebook up 68%. Everybody else down 2%.*
- *Last 20 years has seen disruption to print; next 20 years will see disruption to TV*
- *Traditional TV viewing is declining (average 4 h per day). 86% to 82%*
- *OTT – Modern TV networks growing – Netflix, Amazon Prime, Apple TV, Hulu*
- *iTunes, Netflix dwarf cable networks like AMC*
- *YouTube bigger than CBS in advertising revenues – now into subscriptions plus mobile and social*
- *Netflix is watched more than any other – watch whenever and wherever, on any screen*
- *Old media find niches*
- *Three parts to TV – modern TV networks, access providers (we need more pipes), Traditional TV*
- *networks – pain*
- *Only watch 18 channels per month. Not enough great shows. More shows start, but more dropped in the following year.*
- *Sports starting to see decline*
- *Next Big Thing – smart watches, glasses? Not media consumption devices. Watches mainly used for fitness. Glasses – Snapchat – media construction not consumption. VR and AR – cool. Only 3D TV? But people don't want 3D TV. Important thing is the story. Exception is gaming. VR for storytelling is not needed.*
- *Social video – next Big Thing. Facebook, Snapchat. New kind of story. Sound optional, intimate and conversational. Different to web video. Needs to be in 1–30s. Massive opportunity. 2.5 billion views per month. Social videos can be evocative, entertaining and effective*
- *Social video – Can change behaviour and compel action [6]*

A report by Adweek in 2016 identified that video was taking over digital media, and personalization could be contributing to the development of siloed audiences [7].

Traditional print media, including newspapers, is under challenge from those customers who prefer online content and e-books. Thus media companies are having to adjust to this diversification of requirements [8, 9].

## 8.3   Legal Issues

As noted in Chap. 5, Sect. 5.4, on Digital Libraries, there are ongoing legal issues with regard to Google's copying of books for the Google Digitization Project.

In 1990, Samuelson [10] proposed that the currently established intellectual property law would be severely tested by developments in computing and software. Digital media was defined as –

*intellectual products made available in digital electronic form, whether operational in computers or other machines capable of 'reading' works in digital form* [10]

The following aspects of digital media were identified which required steps to be taken so that intellectual property law could protect works in digital form [10] –

*Six characteristics that will make it difficult for existing categories of intellectual property law to adjust to the protection of works in digital form:*

1. *the ease with which works in digital form can be replicated,*
2. *the ease with they can be transmitted,*
3. *the ease with which they can be modified and manipulated,*
4. *the equivalence of works in digital form,*
5. *the compactness of works in digital form,*
6. *the capacity they have for creating new methods of searching digital space and linking works together* [10].

As noted in Chap. 5, Sect. 5.4 –

On April 18, 2016, the Supreme Court turned down an appeal. *It appears therefore that this decision was currently favoring Google, granting them the right to expand their digital library without violating the law* [11].

However, there may be further appeals, so it is not currently clear what the final outcome will be, given the current problems of seeking to apply laws for traditional physical media to online intangible media.

## 8.4   Digital Rights Management

Digital Rights Management (DRM) prevents unauthorized copying and redistribution of digital media and can also restrict consumers' copying of content which they've purchased [12]. It is implemented by appropriate systems within the digital media content.

**Advocates of DRM Argue that –**

- *It provides protection for the user, modification, and distribution of copyrighted works and the intellectual property within it*
- *It assists the copyright owner in maintaining artistic control over their works*
- *It protects revenue streams from the works* [14]

**Opponents of DRM Argue that –**

- *No evidence DRM helps to prevent copyright infringement*
- *DRM stifles innovation and competition*
- *Content can become permanently inaccessible if the DRM scheme changes*

- *DRM prevents users from backing up copies of CDs and DVDs*
- *DRM prevents libraries lending materials, accessing works in the public domain, or using copyrighted materials for research and education under the fair use doctrine* [14]

In the USA, fair use allows limited use of copyright material without first seeking permission from the copyright holder [15].

It is now illegal in many countries to seek to get round DRM, or distribute information about such activity, and also the creation and distribution of tools to accomplish this. Such laws are part of the United States' Digital Millennium Copyright Act, and the European Union's Copyright Directive [14].

## 8.5   Preservation of Digital Archives

Currently there are long-term issues of digital preservation of information. These are summarized in Chap. 5, Sect. 5.5.

## 8.6   Digital Media Ethics

A writer has raised the question of whether today's ethics in traditional media are sufficient for new media [16], and how professional journalism should use this new media to research and publish stories. Also, are they able to use online text or images posted by citizens on their blogs or social media such as Twitter or Facebook?

Given that traditional media are being transformed by digital technology and its uses and applications, it is good time to visit yet again the ethics of journalism. Many readers have expressed concern about aspects of how traditional journalists have gone about their business, while still respecting the rights and freedoms of the press and the need to protect these in the overall interests of citizens and governments.

## 8.7   Content Delivery Networks

Many users now integrate their user requirements with data and information storage on the Internet, so clearly need continuous access to their web sites and storage vehicles via their Internet Service Provider. Thus many companies are seeking to add value to their content services by offering cloud storage. Often it is free of charge to those with modest requirements and only increasing to a monthly rate for those with high requirements, typically corporate users. Some even offer super computing services via the cloud for compute-intensive requirements.

Google has one of the fastest and most accurate search algorithms. By pre-storing its search results, it is able to deliver a result to a query almost instantaneously and within the 1–2 s response time identified many years ago as a requirement to maintain user interest [17].

Google's fast response time also depends on its content delivery network and it is known to have one of the largest and complex networks which is still able to respond very quickly despite the high volumes of information it has to process generated by an estimated 40,000 global searches per sec (i.e. 3.5 billion per day). To this should be added its own searches for new information that is constantly being added to the Internet – to ensure its databases that are accessed by user-searches are kept fully up to date [18].

## 8.8   Golden Rules of Interface Design

Shneiderman's 8 Golden Rules of Interface Design [19] are widely accepted as good practice for software designers, applications developers, and users. A number of these place an onus on the system designer – such as to provide responses to errors that are simple and appropriate. Clearly these also depend on the system providing a timely response, which in turn requires timely responses from the content provider on the Internet for user applications accessing their content. Connections between these rules and earlier work by Foley and Wallace on natural graphic man-machine communication [20] may be noted.

## Further Reading

Ess, C.: Digital Media Ethics. Polity Press, Cambridge (2009)

Friend, C., Singer, J.: Online Journalism Ethics: Traditions and Transitions. M. E. Sharpe, Armonk (2007)

Lemley, M.A., Menell, P.S., Merges, R.P., Samuelson, P.: Software and Internet Law. Aspen Publishers, New York (2006)

Samuelson, P.: Intellectual Property in the Age of Universal Access. Association for Computing Machinery, New York (1999). http://dl.acm.org/citation.cfm?id=318536&picked=prox

Sourin, A., Earnshaw, R.A., Gavrilova, M.L., Sourina, O.O.: Problems of Human-Computer Interaction in Cyberworlds. Transactions on Computational Science XXVIII, vol. 9590, pp. 1–22. Springer (2016). http://link.springer.com/book/10.1007/978-3-662-53090-0

Vince, J.A., Earnshaw, R.A. (eds.): Digital Media: The Future, pp. 312. Springer, London. ISBN: 1-85233-246-8. (2000). http://www.springer.com/social+sciences/book/978-1-85233-246-4 http://www.springer.com/gb/book/9781852332464

# Web Sites

Issues raised by Media Ownership. https://www.slideshare.net/robertclackmedia/issues-raised-by-media-ownership

Predictions on the Future of Digital Media. https://techcrunch.com/gallery/predictions-on-the-future-of-digital-media/slide/1/

# References

1. https://www.ted.com/speakers/alan_kay
2. https://phys.org/news/2015-08-silicon-limits-power-electronics-revolution.html; https://arstechnica.co.uk/gadgets/2016/07/itrs-roadmap-2021-moores-law/; https://www.technologyreview.com/s/600716/intel-chips-will-have-to-sacrifice-speed-gains-for-energy-savings/
3. http://www.marketingcharts.com/television/are-young-people-watching-less-tv-24817/; http://mediakix.com/2016/10/top-10-tv-advertising-statistics-showing-decline/#gs.YU3x7EM
4. http://uk.businessinsider.com/traditional-tv-is-in-decline-2015-8?r=US&IR=T
5. http://uk.businessinsider.com/here-is-emarketers-guide-to-the-future-of-digital-media-2017-1
6. http://uk.businessinsider.com/future-of-digital-media-bi-intelligence-henry-blodget-ignition-2016-12?r=US&IR=T; http://uk.businessinsider.com/here-is-emarketers-guide-to-the-future-of-digital-media-2017-1
7. http://www.adweek.com/digital/the-future-of-digital-media-visual-media-and-niche-audiences-report/
8. Lunden, K.: The Death of Print? The Challenges and Opportunities facing the Print Media on the Web. Reuters Institute for the Study of Journalism. University of Oxford, Oxford (2009). https://reutersinstitute.politics.ox.ac.uk/sites/default/files/The%20Death%20of%20Print%20-%20The%20Challenges%20and%20Opportunities%20facing%20the%20Print%20Media%20on%20the%20Web.pdf
9. Saperstein, T.: The future of print: newspapers struggle to survive in the age of technology. Harvard Political Review (December 6, 2014). http://harvardpolitics.com/covers/future-print-newspapers-struggle-survive-age-technology/
10. http://scholarship.law.berkeley.edu/cgi/viewcontent.cgi?article=1245&context=facpubs; https://www.law.berkeley.edu/our-faculty/faculty-profiles/pamela-samuelson/; http://people.ischool.berkeley.edu/~pam/papers.html; https://en.wikipedia.org/wiki/Pamela_Samuelson
11. https://en.wikipedia.org/wiki/Google_Book_Search_Settlement_Agreement; https://en.wikipedia.org/wiki/Google_Books; https://phys.org/news/2016-04-supreme-court-google--online-library.html
12. http://searchcio.techtarget.com/definition/digital-rights-management. There are pros and cons to DRM [13]
13. http://www.cbc.ca/news/technology/the-pros-cons-and-future-of-drm-1.785237
14. https://en.wikipedia.org/wiki/Digital_rights_management
15. https://en.wikipedia.org/wiki/Fair_use
16. Ward, S.J.A.: Digital Media Ethics. Center for Journalism Ethics. University of Wisconsin-Madison, USA https://ethics.journalism.wisc.edu/resources/digital-media-ethics/; https://www.mediaethicsmagazine.com/index.php/browse-back-issues/144-fall-2012/3998645-concept-media-ethics-in-the-digital-age
17. Shneiderman, B.: Response time and display rate in human performance with computers. ACM Comput. Surv. 16(3) (September 1984). https://www.cs.umd.edu/~ben/papers/Shneiderman1984Response.pdf; https://www.nngroup.com/articles/response-times-3-important-limits/; http://collecter.org/archives/2000_April/03.pdf

18. https://en.wikipedia.org/wiki/Google_Data_Centers; https://en.wikipedia.org/wiki/Content_delivery_network
19. https://faculty.washington.edu/jtenenbg/courses/360/f04/sessions/schneidermanGoldenRules.html; https://www.cs.umd.edu/users/ben/goldenrules.html; https://www.interaction-design.org/literature/article/shneiderman-s-eight-golden-rules-will-help-you-design-better-interfaces
20. Foley, J.D., Wallace, V.L.: The art of natural graphic man-machine conversation. Proc. IEEE. 62, 462–471 (1974). http://ieeexplore.ieee.org/document/1451380/. doi:10.1109/PROC.1974.9450

# Rationale for Bibliographic References

This bibliography contains additional references for readers who wish to study particular areas in more detail than that provided in the Further Reading and References at the end of each chapter. Readers should note that appropriate Further Reading for each chapter is included at the end of each chapter and this bibliography does not duplicate these references. Note that the reference numbers 1–61 are not referred to in the main text as this is a list of books which is additional reading to that referred to directly in the book, and provides more detail in each of the topic areas below.

## Bibliography

### *Image Manipulation*

1. Wolper, V.E.: Photograph Restoration and Enhancement Using Adobe Photoshop, p. 350. Mercury Learning and Information (2013)
2. Ctein: Digital Restoration from Start to Finish, p. 448. Focal Press, Waltham (2010)
3. Faulkner, A., Chavez, C.: Adobe Photoshop CC Classroom in a Book (2017 Release), p. 400. Adobe, San Jose (2016)
4. Jago, M.: Adobe Premiere Pro CC Classroom in a Book (2017 Release), p. 480. Adobe, San Jose (2017)
5. Kelby, S.: The Adobe Photoshop CC Book for Digital Photographers 2017, p. 360. New Riders, San Francisco (2016)
6. Kelby, S.: How Do I Do that in Lightroom?: The Quickest Ways to Do the Things You Want to Do Right Now! , p. 272. Rocky Nook, San Rafael (2015)
7. Beck, T.S.: Shaping Images: Scholarly Perspectives on Image Manipulation, p. 217. De Gruyter Saur, Munich (2016)
8. Burns, S.: 3D Photoshop for Creative Professionals: Interactive Guide for Creating 3D Art, p. 310. Focal Press, Waltham (2016)
9. Ahearn, L.: 3D Game Textures: Create Professional Game Art using Photoshop, p. 412. A. K. Peters/CRC Press, Natick (2016)

© The Author(s) 2017

R. Earnshaw, *State of the Art in Digital Media and Applications*, SpringerBriefs in Computer Science, DOI 10.1007/978-3-319-61409-0

10. Anatomy for 3D Artists, p. 288. 3DTotal Publishing (2015)
11. Beginner's Guide to Character Creation in Maya, p. 272. 3DTotal Publishing (2015)
12. Beginner's Guide to Digital Painting in Photoshop, p. 244. 3DTotal Publishing (2012)
13. Purse, L.: Digital Imaging in Popular Cinema, p. 208. Edinburgh University Press, Edinburgh (2013)
14. Derakhshani, D.: Introducing Autodesk Maya 2016, p. 624. Sybex, Hoboken (2015)

## Multimedia

15. Li, Z., Drew, M.S., Liu, J.: Fundamentals of Multimedia, p. 752. Springer, Cham (2014)

## Image Processing

16. Tanimoto, S.L.: An Interdisciplinary Introduction to Image Processing: Pixels, Numbers, and Programs, p. 534. MIT Press, Cambridge, MA (2012)
17. Chityala, R., Pudipeddi, S.: Image Processing and Acquisition using Python, p. 390. Chapman and Hall/CRC, London (2014)
18. Gonzalez, R.C., Woods, R.E.: Digital Image Processing, p. 1184. Pearson, London (2017)
19. Russ, J.C., Neal, F.B.: The Image Processing Handbook, p. 1053. CRC Press, Boca Raton (2015)
20. Russ J.C.: The Image Processing Cookbook, p. 96. CreateSpace Independent Publishing Platform (2016)
21. Gonzalez, R.C., Eddins, S.L., Woods, R.E.: Digital Image Processing using MATLAB, p. 827. Gatesmark Publishing, London (2009)
22. Solomon, C., Breckon, T.: Fundamentals of Digital Image Processing: A Practical Approach with Examples in MATLAB, p. 344. Wiley-Blackwell, Hoboken (2010)
23. Shukla, K.K., Prasad, M.V.: Lossy Image Compression: Domain Decomposition-Based Algorithms, p. 104. Springer, London (2011)
24. Corke, P.: Robotics, Vision and Control: Fundamental Algorithms in MATLAB, p. 570. Springer, Berlin (2011)
25. Attaway, S.: MATLAB: A Practical Introduction to Programming and Problem Solving, p. 560. Butterworth-Heinemann, Oxford (2013)

## Image Compression

26. Joshi, M.A., Raval, M.S., Dandawate, Y.H., Joshi, K.R., Metkar, S.P.: Image and Video Compression: Fundamentals, Techniques, and Applications, p. 236. Chapman and Hall/CRC, London (2014)
27. Thyagarajan, K.S.: Still Image and Video Compression with MATLAB, p. 428. Wiley-Blackwell, Hoboken (2010)
28. McAndrew, A.: A Computational Introduction to Digital Image Processing, p. 551. Chapman and Hall/CRC, London (2015)
29. Hlavac, V., Sonka, M., Boyle, R.: Image Processing, Analysis, and Machine Vision, p. 920. CL Engineering. (2014)

30. Bendell, C., Kadlec, T., Weiss, Y., Podjarny, G., Doyle, N., McCall, M.: High Performance Images: Shrink, Load, and deliver Images for Speed, p. 354. O'Reilly, Sebastopol (2016)
31. Bocharova, I.: Compression for Multimedia, p. 280. Cambridge University Press, Cambridge (2009)
32. Woods, J.W.: Multidimensional Signal, Image and Video Processing and Coding, p. 616. Academic, Cambridge, MA (2011)
33. Pearlman, W.A.: Wavelet Image Compression, p. 90. Morgan and Claypool Publishers, San Rafael (2013)
34. Jindal, R.: Image Compression Techniques: An Analysis: Evaluation using Higher Order Metrics, p. 84. LAP Lambert Academic Publishing, Saarbrucken (2017)

## Image Standards

35. WDL Digital Image Standards https://project.wdl.org/standards/imagestandards.html
36. A Resource List for Standards Related to Digital Imaging of Print, Graphic, and Pictorial Materials http://www.digitizationguidelines.gov/guidelines/digitize-standards.html
37. Graphics and Image Standards for the Web https://energy.gov/eere/communicationstandards/graphics-and-image-standards-web
38. Image File Formats https://en.wikipedia.org/wiki/Image_file_formats
39. Standard Image Sizes http://www.fileformat.info/tip/web/imagesize.htm
40. Multimedia Standards http://www.dtic.upf.edu/~jblat/material/doctorat/multimedia_standards.html
41. Moving Picture Experts Group https://en.wikipedia.org/wiki/Moving_Picture_Experts_Group
42. IEEE Images and Multimedia https://www.ieee.org/about/webteam/styleguide/images_multimedia.html
43. JPEG https://en.wikipedia.org/wiki/JPEG.; https://jpeg.org/; https://web.cs.wpi.edu/~kal/elecdoc/MMjpeg.html

## Special Effects

44. McClean, S.: Digital Storytelling: The Narrative Power of Visual Effects in Film, p. 320. MIT Press, Cambridge, MA (2008)
45. Prince, S.: Digital Visual Effects in Cinema: The Seduction of Reality, p. 256. Rutgers University Press, Rutgers (2012)
46. Whissel, K.: Spectacular Digital Effects: CGI and Contemporary Cinema, p. 224. Duke University Press, Durham (2014)
47. North, D., Rehak, R., Duffy, M.S. (eds.): Special Effects: New Histories, Theories, Contexts, p. 304. British Film Institute, London (2015)
48. Keil, C., Keil, W.: Editing and Special/Visual Effects: Behind the Silver Screen – A Modern History of Filmmaking, p. 256. I.B. Tauris, London (2016)
49. Rickitt, R.: Special Effects: The History and Technique, p. 318. Virgin Books, London (2000)
50. Brinkmann, R.: The Art and Science of Digital Compositing: Techniques for Visual Effects, Animation and Motion Graphics, p. 704. Morgan Kaufmann, Burlington (2008)
51. Wright, S.: Digital Compositing for Film and Video, p. 512. Focal Press, Waltham (2010)
52. Pohlmann, K.C.: Principles of Digital Audio, p. 816. McGraw-Hill Education, New York (2010)

## *Modeling*

53. Gahan, A.: 3ds Max Modeling for Games: Insider's Guide to Game Character, Vehicle, and Environment Modeling: Vol 1, p. 480. Focal Press, Waltham (2011a)
54. Gahan, A.: 3ds Max Modeling for Games: Insider's Guide to Stylized Modeling: 2, p. 380. Focal Press, Waltham (2011b)
55. Brooker, D.: Essential CG Lighting Techniques with 3ds Max, p. 416. Focal Press, Waltham (2008)
56. Birn, J.: Digital Lighting and Rendering, p. 464. New Riders, San Francisco (2013)
57. Vaughan, W.: Digital Modeling, p. 432. New Riders, San Francisco (2013)

## *Medical Imaging*

58. Shephard, C.T.: Radiographic Image Production and Manipulation, p. 416. McGraw-Hill Education/Medical, New York (2002)

## *Robotics*

59. Siegwart, R., Nourbakhsh, I.R., Scaramuzza, D.: Introduction to Autonomous Mobile Robots, p. 488. MIT Press, Cambridge, MA (2011)
60. Choset, H., Lynch, K.M., Kantor, G., Burgard, W., Kavraki, L.E., Thrun, S.: Principles of Robot Motion: Theory, Algorithms, and Implementations, p. 550. MIT Press, Cambridge, MA (2005)
61. Thrun, S., Burgard, W., Fox, D.: Probabilistic Robotics, p. 668. MIT Press, Cambridge, MA (2005)